EARTH, OUR HOME:
BIBLICAL WITNESS IN THE HEBREW SCRIPTURES

D1400759

SOR JUANA PRESS

Sor Juana Press is a project of Santuario Sisterfarm, a nonprofit organization rooted in the Texas Hill Country and grounded in the rich multi-cultural legacy of the Borderlands. Founded in 2002, Santuario Sisterfarm inspirits the work of transforming human relationships with Earth and other humans by moving from dominance to co-creative partnerships, drawing on insights from wisdom traditions, nature, the new science, and women's ways. Santuario Sisterfarm advances its mission by cultivating diversity—biodiversity and cultural diversity.

Sor Juana Press is dedicated to publishing the works of women—particularly women of color and women religious—on topics rooted in women's spirituality and relationship with Earth, *la Tierra, nuestra madre*.

The Press invokes the name and honors the memory of Sor Juana Inés de la Cruz (1648-1695), a Mexican nun, scholar, poet, playwright, musician, and scientist—a woman with a *sed de conocer* (a thirst for knowing)—who was silenced for advocating women's education. She is the first writer in the Americas to speak out in favor of a woman's right to learn and express concern about human depredation of the environment.

Other Books in the "Dominican Women on Earth" Series

EARTH SPIRITUALITY: IN THE CATHOLIC AND DOMINICAN TRADITIONS
by Sharon Therese Zayac, O.P. (Issue No. 1, June 2003).

PERMACULTURE: FINDING OUR OWN VINES AND FIG TREES
by Carol Coston, O.P. (Issue No. 2, August 2003).

EARTH, OUR HOME:
BIBLICAL WITNESS IN THE HEBREW SCRIPTURES

Sarah Ann Sharkey, O.P.

CONVERSATIO
Dominican Women on Earth

Issue No.3   February 2004

SOR JUANA PRESS

© 2004 Sor Juana Press

Edited by Elise D. García and Carol Coston, O.P.

Cover photo: Image courtesy of Earth Sciences and Image Analysis
Laboratory, NASA Johnson Space Center. "Astronaut Photography
of Earth—Quick View."
<http://eol.jsc.nasa.gov/scripts/sseop/QuickView.pl?directory=ISD&I
D=STS108-717-93>

Book and cover design by Susan E. Klein of Sister Creek Studios, San
Antonio, Texas. (www.sistercreekstudios.com)

Printed by Crumrine Printers, Inc., San Antonio, Texas

Properly footnoted quotations of up to 500 sequential words may be
used without permission. For longer quotations, please write to
Sor Juana Press for permission. Mailing address: Sor Juana Press,
28 Hein Road, Boerne, Texas 78006

This book is printed with soy inks on 100% post-consumer recycled
paper, processed chorine-free, supplied by Dolphin Blue, a Dallas,
Texas-based company specializing in environmentally responsible
office products. (www.dolphinblue.com)

ISBN 0-9740243-2-5
ISSN 1543-978X

www.santuariosisterfarm.org

TABLE OF CONTENTS

ABOUT THE AUTHOR

Sarah Ann Sharkey, O.P., an Adrian (Michigan) Dominican Sister, is presently serving on the faculty of Oblate School of Theology in San Antonio, Texas, as a professor in the department of Biblical Studies. Before going to Oblate in 1995, she served on the academic and formation faculties of St. Mary's Seminary and University in Baltimore, Maryland, for thirteen years. In her twenty-plus years of instructing on the graduate and doctoral levels, it has been important to Sarah to teach in settings where students not only acquire a firm and responsible academic foundation in biblical studies but also discover a love for the Word of God that will enrich their spiritual and ministerial lives, as well as the lives of those with whom they minister. In addition to teaching Scripture courses at Oblate, Sarah is a presenter in a variety of Oblate's programs: Continuing Education Programs, the Lay Ministry Institute, and Ministry to Ministers sabbatical program for women and men religious. She welcomes opportunities to provide adult education programs and workshops on the study of the Bible (especially on topics of biblical justice, ecology, and women) at the parish, diocesan, and national levels. Sarah particularly delights in sharing the Word with her own Adrian Dominican sisters. In her own educational history, Sarah earned an M.A. in Biblical Studies from Union Theological Seminary/Columbia University in 1972 and a Ph.D. in Biblical Studies at The Catholic University of America in 1986. From 1972-76, Sarah served as Director of Initial Formation for the Adrian Dominican Congregation.

SHARING THE JOURNEY

It has been said that when one talks about creation, language soars. As I have opened the cover of my Bible again and again with the writing of this "little book," I have encountered language that could hardly stay fixed on the page. It has been a wonderful experience. So I begin this personal reflection by thanking Elise D. García and Carol Coston, O.P. of Santuario Sisterfarm, where all creation is reverenced, for the invitation to stand before the marvel of creation with the Word of God as my companion and guide in this project.

In taking a walk down memory lane, I realize that nature/creation has always been a precious part of my life. I call Texas my home state. My German ancestors landed on its coastline some 150 years ago. My mother grew up in a small rural Texas town. I spent the first twelve years of my life and these last eight years in Texas. I have clear memories of growing up in the Panhandle of the state where hot summers and blizzardy winters were the norm. Tumble weeds blew down the streets and sand filled up the space between window and screen when the winds blew. I recall our little house and the yard—the roses on the trellis that I got to cut for my Dad's birthday in June; beautiful irises in Mother's garden; a tall lilac hedge across the whole backyard; honeysuckle that announced itself with its sweet, soothing smell before you saw it.

I always had a cat with names such as Sandy and Blacky. How important these felines were to me as companions since I was an only child! I can remember cold winter nights tucked in bed hearing my Dad outside calling the  cat to come in and I recall standing in the kitchen grinning, watching my cat eat my Mother's unbaked tuna-noodle casserole on the table while she was out hanging clothes in the sunshine. In those early years, we went to visit family in New Mexico and I experienced for the first time the beauty of mountains and desert meeting.

During my high school years and in religious community life, I have lived in a number of parts of this country. The daffodils and forsythia in all their yellow and white splendor greeted me every spring in South Carolina and Maryland and Washington, D.C., followed by the dogwood and incredibly lovely azaleas. And I loved the season of fall with its rich, vibrant changing colors. I have taken pleasure in the tropical flora of Florida and the cornfields of Michigan. I experienced the peace and power of the Atlantic Ocean and Gulf of Mexico when I lived near these great bodies of water.

During two years of study in New York City, the window in my small room at Corpus Christi Convent on 121st Street presented a view of the brick wall of the building next door. Somewhere in upper Manhattan I found a little green plant and that plant sat on my windowsill for those two years—such a faithful little friend!

Now here in San Antonio, I am gratefully aware of the precious beauty of wild flowers and trees and the practice of xeriscaping that many here adopt. During the long hot summers, one also comes to know the concern about the level of water in the Edwards Aquifer that is stretched in its capacity to take care of us all and ozone action alert days when the driving of cars and use of gasoline mowers are strongly discouraged. When weather fronts converge from the north and west and moisture flows in from the Gulf, I have seen our quiet residential streets flood with torrents of water sweeping cars away effortlessly—a lesson in the power of nature.

For years I lived without animal companions in convents and community houses. I must say it always seemed that something was missing. But now they are back! My dear friend and sister in community, Melba Beine, and I have provided a haven for homeless and sometimes abused cats over the years. Melba says there is a sign in front of our little house visible only to felines that reads "good eats here." Fred, Sunny, and Puff now grace our home. Their gratitude and faithfulness and companionship just cannot be beat. Opening our door to them has opened the door to a bit of God's creation, life has walked in, and we have not regretted our efforts for one moment.

Once I reached school age in Amarillo, Texas, my parents enrolled me at St. Mary's Academy where I met the Sisters of Charity of the Incarnate Word. Although I grew to love school life later on, that first year was filled with home-sickness even though home was only three miles away. In school, I can remember standing by my desk and reciting answers to Baltimore Catechism questions and getting stars on the chart for my efforts. I can say that I "loved" God but that God was distant, omniscient, and almighty as the Catechism stated. Early on, I con-cluded that if I was "a good girl," I would please this God and so I tried to become that kind of child.

My Dad's job took us to Birmingham, Alabama, when I was high school age. I look back on those years in Birmingham and at John Carroll High School (Benedictine Sisters) as some of the happiest of my life. I had such good friends and we enjoyed beings teens in the 1950s. In my senior year, my ordered world began to shift. I spoke to a priest in

Birmingham and told him that I thought I had a "vocation" to religious life. He told me that he knew just the community for me (a community previously 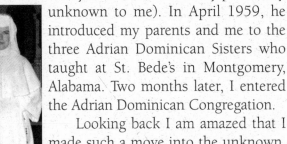 unknown to me). In April 1959, he introduced my parents and me to the three Adrian Dominican Sisters who taught at St. Bede's in Montgomery, Alabama. Two months later, I entered the Adrian Dominican Congregation.

Looking back I am amazed that I made such a move into the unknown, but I have never regretted a minute of that decision. I believed that it was all part of "God's will," and that God, although still a distant God, had a plan for me that I felt compelled to follow.

During the next ten years, I found myself teaching young children in Aiken, South Carolina, and in Ft. Walton Beach, Ft. Lauderdale, and Vero Beach in Florida. I enjoyed teaching even though the number of children in the classrooms (over sixty at times) was staggering. In turn, I asked those children to stand next to their desks to recite answers to Catechism questions and God seemed to watch over the more or less ordered life of Church and religious community. Vatican II would once again shake my ordered world.

In 1970, in the early years of renewal in the Church and religious life, I went to New York City and began two exciting years of living in that city and studying Scripture at Union Theological Seminary. Having been raised on the Baltimore Catechism, I had a lot of "catching up" to do in getting to know the Bible. Those were dramatic years in terms of my experience of God. I discovered in the pages of the Bible a God who "drew near" to human beings in history, a God who walked with people on journeys of liberation as well as exile, a God who had drawn so near that this God was fleshed out in my humanness.

To discover this human side of God after knowing God as only divine was meaningful to me beyond words. During those same years, we began to talk much more about the "Spirit" (in place of the "Holy Ghost") as the life-giving, energizing, prophetic force in our midst and I began to experience that Spirit together with others as we moved through those exciting and unsettling years of renewal.

Studies in Scripture continued a few years later at the Catholic University of America in Washington, D.C. I am profoundly grateful to my Congregation for making the study experiences possible. The study of the Word of God has put me in close touch with the Dominican charism of preaching and teaching the Word at St. Mary's Seminary in Baltimore, Maryland, for thirteen years and at Oblate School of Theology in San Antonio, Texas, for over eight years.

Out of the study and teaching have come my passion and commitment to biblical justice.

In the 1980s, I was invited to join a retreat team created by Walter Burghardt, S.J. that conducts the "Just Word" retreats. My eyes were opened to the differences between biblical justice and our western understanding of justice. I discovered that the Word of God before me defined justice as right relationship between God and humankind and the Earth/land and all its creatures. In the first years of this discovery, I focused on social justice with an emphasis on impoverished and marginalized human beings. However, in recent years, the latter part of the definition of biblical justice that refers to right relationship with the Earth/creation has had a profound impact on me and never ceases to inspire me. I weave it into my teaching, offer a course on "Biblical Justice," and give presentations on the topic whenever I have the opportunity.

This insight also has helped me appreciate the interconnectedness of my Congregation's Vision Statements, addressing those who are impoverished, women, racism, and ecology in the context of the Dominican charism. I am now aware that all parts of God's creation are linked; if one part suffers, all suffer. If one part rejoices, we all rejoice. I spent years feeling stretched in too many directions. How could I ever address all these Congregational issues? Now I understand that if I address one piece of the mosaic, all other pieces are affected. I am more focused and feel ever so much more at peace.

Somehow as I reflect on the mini-life story above, I realize that I feel that everything I hold dear has come together or, perhaps, a better way to say this is that "I have come home." The God I love, the God who walks with me day in and day out, is the God I find everywhere I turn—in friends and family and my Dominican sisters, in the faces of the disenfranchised and marginalized, in those who suffer and despair, in those who smile throughout the struggle, in the trees outside my window and the bluebonnets and Indian paintbrush wildflowers that bedeck the

 Texas Hill Country in spring, in the floods and remnants of hurricanes that pass through here, in Fred, Sunny, and Puff who share our home, in the birds and squirrels who come to dine daily. When I take a moment to reflect, I am awestruck as I walk in the presence of a God who has set the cosmos, this marvelous creation, in motion and loves it all so dearly and never, ever gives up on what was made "good" in the beginning.

As I experience well being, I am also aware of the crisis that Earth is experiencing as we humans give much too little thought to her well-being. This awareness prods me to do what I can in my corner of creation to re-establish biblical justice. I am so glad to say that along the way I am meeting sisters and brothers who share the vision and the challenge.

In writing about creation and the Word of God, gratitude is a spontaneous response. It was so for Israel and the early Christians and it is so today. This whole endeavor calls me to say thanks to a very long list of those who have helped me come to this moment and deepen my love for creation and my passion for its well being especially as I understand it in the context of the Judeo-Christian biblical tradition. I will make the written list short and hold everyone else in my heart.

Thank you …

to my parents, Marceline and Paul, who took my hand and led me into the world and showed me its wonders.

to Melba, my dear friend and Adrian Dominican sister in community and physician from the Midwest, who knows and cares for Earth and all her creatures (human and other-than-human) so compassionately and gently and faithfully.

to Rosemary Ferguson who, as prioress of the Adrian Dominican Congregation, opened the way for me to study Scripture over thirty years ago. Little did I realize how that opportunity would shape and give joy to my life as a Dominican, a student of the Word, a student of creation.

to the Missionary Oblates of Mary Immaculate with whom I minister. These committed men have resolved to promote the "integrity of creation" and that is being realized at Oblate School of Theology.

to Mary Ellen Leciejewski and Kathy Erard, two Adrian Dominican friends, who have been my mentors for years as they have pointed prophetically to the critical importance of the study of ecology and the conversion of lifestyle it demands, two women who live their commitment day in and day out.

to Joan Marie Weithman, my dear friend of forty-four years in the Congregation. One of our favorite topics of conversation is how much animals do for us as they help to heal us and teach us what faithfulness is all about. Joan and I hope our retirement center in Adrian has live-in pets by the time we arrive on the doorstep.

to Nancyann Turner, a constant friend and Adrian Dominican, who has opened the beauty of creation to the wounded and impoverished through her gifts of artistic expression. Nancyann also tends Earth with care and knows how all this connects.

to Angharad Rees, a dear and dedicated woman, who combines her ministry of nursing and healing humans with care of abandoned and abused animals at Safe Harbour refuge.

to my cousin Sam, dear, good woman, who opens her door in hospitality to all. Sam has taken home many of God's little broken creatures and always has room for one more dog or cat. In that she reflects God's own care.

and to our cats, B.G., Sootie Foot, and Zephyr; Tippy, Stormy, and Licorice; and Fred, Sunny and Puff for coming to visit and deciding to stay.

Thank you.

INTRODUCTION

I spent the summer traveling; I got half way across my backyard.

-Louis Agassiz, scientist (1807-1873)

On an early summer day, two small young doves, having recently exited the nest, wandered around our front yard apparently eager to explore. Their parents flew overhead—protecting, urging, encouraging their young whose wings had not yet borne them into the air. Sunny ("Sunshine"), one of our three rescued cats, contemplated the scene. Finally, he squelched his predatory instinct (perhaps because I had my eye on him), turned, and wandered off for a nap. I thanked Sunny.

Two days later I walked very close to one of the young doves before seeing it. The little one stretched those small wings, lifted off the ground, and flew all of six feet. One of the parents quickly landed on the ground next to its offspring while the other parent circled and came to rest in a tree overhead. The next day, we trust they joined the 100-plus birds and family of squirrels who come to dine daily in our backyard. Truly a walk in the yard yields the wonders of creation.

An Overview

In this "little book" about caring for Earth, our home, we will listen to millennia-old voices that speak from the pages of Scripture about creation, as well as to voices of contemporary theologians who reflect on the biblical Word and ecology. If we listen closely, we may well hear an urgent invitation to add our voices to those who speak prophetically in warning about ecological disaster and, at the same time, offer hope for Earth and the common good of all her inhabitants.

First, let us take a brief look at where we are today in relation to the topic of ecology and our relationship to Earth. A review of the word "ecology" tells us that *eco* comes from the Greek *oikos* ("household") and *logy* from *logos* ("word" or "expression"). Ecology is then the "word of the household." D. H. Lawrence in the poem "Pax" gives "ecology" poetic expression:

All that matters is to be at one with the living God
to be a creature in the house of the God of life.
Like a cat asleep on a chair

at peace, in peace
and at one with the master of the house,
  with the mistress,
at home, at home in the house of the living,
sleeping on the hearth, and yawning before
  the fire.

Sleeping on the hearth of the living world,
yawning at home before the fire of life,
feeling the presence of the living God
like a great reassurance,
a deep calm in the heart.[1]

The peacefulness conveyed by Lawrence's poem and experienced with the family of doves and Sunny, the cat, however, has to be set in a larger context that has both positive and negative ecological aspects. On the positive side, we come to appreciate and marvel at the "new creation story" that contemporary science reveals. It is a story of a world that, as theologian Elizabeth A. Johnson, C.S.J. writes, is "unimaginably old, large, dynamic, and organic. When filtered through the eyes of faith, it reveals a Creator Spirit initiating, upholding, moving, vivifying, and playing in a world that grows increasingly bright and complex—truly the Giver of Life."[2] This new creation story teaches us that while Earth is our home and has instrumental value for human use, "it is more than just a stage or backdrop for the human drama of

15

redemption; rather, it is a marvelous creation in its own right, loved by God for itself, saved by Christ, destined for eternal life in the new creation. It has its own intrinsic value."[3]

On the negative side, awareness grows that Earth is in serious trouble. In the past, human sin was understood to cause division and suffering within the human community. Now, we understand that sin inflicts suffering on all creation. Elizabeth Johnson provides concrete facts that may jar us: 20% of Earth's people in rich nations use 75% of the world's resources and produce 80% of the world's waste. In 1950 the world numbered two billion people; at the turn of the millennium it numbered six billion. By the year 2030 there will be ten billion people on the planet. The carrying capacity of Earth is being exhausted by this growth. Earth cannot regenerate resources at the rate that we are using them. Widespread destruction of ecosystems leads to the extinction of the lives that thrive in these habitats. By a conservative estimate, in the last quarter of the twentieth century, 20% of all living species has gone extinct. When these living beings, these magnificent plants and animals, go extinct, they never come back again.[4] And on rush the facts that wrench us out of our comfortable and secure ways of thinking and living.

In this postmodern period we are realizing that the earlier outlook of dominance of human control over nature with little concern about limits has led to a catastrophic situation regarding the state of Earth, her human and non-human inhabitants, and her resources. We are now realizing that anthropocentrism is problematic when humans see themselves as the only subjects and regard other creatures as objects with no inherent value, created merely to serve human needs. Greed, over-consumption, unbridled individualism, and profit-driven economic systems are wreaking havoc with Earth and all she holds.

This ecological crisis puts before us a moral challenge and responsibility for decision-making that has far-reaching implications. We are called upon to engage in a radical shift in the way we see ourselves in relationship with the rest of creation. The "integrity of creation," "web of life," and "community of life" are current expressions that acknowledge the interrelatedness of our vast ecosystem. We are all in this together. Everything is connected to everything else. We live in an incredibly dynamic, complex universe that is constantly changing. To become ecologically literate is to open ourselves to seeing and feeling the world differently. Once we begin to appreciate this interconnectedness, we have little choice but to adjust our theological and spiritual outlooks, change our lifestyles in response to living in a world with limits, and speak out as prophetic preachers on behalf of justice and God's plan for this world, the whole of creation.

COMPLEXITY OF THE PROBLEM

The ecological crisis is not a single, isolated situation but rather a massive mosaic of intertwined problems that adversely affects all parts of creation. *All* creation is groaning (Rom 8:22). The well being of human beings is deeply connected with the well being of the rest of creation and vice-versa. We are part of the natural world, not separate from it. If one strand of the "web of life" is harmed, the whole web suffers and is weakened. The cry of humans who are impoverished must be heard alongside the cry of Earth. It is imperative that ecological sustainability and justice in the face of human oppression not be alternative concerns that are pitted against each other. The logic that exploits humans and subjects peoples to the interests of the few rich and powerful is the same logic that devastates Earth and plunders her wealth. Humans have shown that they can commit not only homicide and ethnocide, but biocide and geocide as well.

Tensions, however, do exist between "eco-justice" and "social justice."[5] In 1998, Auburn and Union Theological Seminaries hosted a major conference on Ecology and Social Justice titled "Ecumenical Earth." For the conference, 170 participants from ten countries were brought together and participated in theological reflection that began with a variety of voices addressing crucial issues:

• Russell Botman from South Africa stated that "right now in South Africa ecological and justice concerns continue to be segregated. White people are concerned only about the ecological issues in white areas."

• Korean feminist theologian Chung Hyun Kyung explained that Third World people feel that First World people commit "environmental fascism" when "you now want to regulate the resources you used to get rich, so we can't develop. And First World people accuse the Third World of 'environmental terrorism' when we destroy our forests, our environment, our wetlands to develop." It is an ideological impasse to work through.

• African-American theologian James Cone stated that many African Americans think that "white people care more about the endangered whale than they do about the survival of young Blacks in our nation's cities." At the same time, he said, a typical comment of ecologists is: "Blacks don't care about the environment." Cone continued: "Justice fighters for Blacks and the earth have tended to ignore each other.... Their separation is unfortunate because they are fighting the same enemy—human beings' domination of each other and nature." But Cone believes the separation is narrowing because of the growing awareness "that ecology touches every sphere of human existence. What good is it to eliminate racism if we are not around to enjoy a racist-free environment?"

• Feminist ethicist Beverly Harrison pointed out that many progressive Latin American women have begun to call themselves "eco-justice feminists" to indicate how seriously they take the environmental concern and to distance themselves somewhat from liberation theology, which they still find to have a male bias.

• Vernice Miller of the Natural Resources Defense Council stated: "Among a variety of indicators, race was the best predictor of the location of hazardous waste facilities in the United States." She noted that of the nation's commercial hazardous waste landfill capacity, 40% was in three predominantly African-American and Latino communities.

• Womanist theologian Delores Williams suggested that the sin of our day is much less the "alienation" from God and each other stressed a generation ago; rather the sin of our day is "blasphemy," our "contempt and lack of reverence for that which is sacred and sustainable. We have sinned by violating the earth and other communities."[6]

We may well add our own experiences and the tensions we have encountered. It is clear that the problems centered in this ecological crisis are numerous, complex, yet interrelated. The solutions, in turn, will be multi-faceted yet interconnected. Looking for solutions cannot be put off for another day. The crisis requires urgent response.

WHERE DO WE TURN FOR HELP?

One positive consequence of a crisis is that it wakes us up and causes us to look anew at what we may be taking for granted. It encourages us to consider our own participation in causing the problem and that can lead to transforming decisions in our lives. While we may be committed to the future and the discovery of new and innovative solutions, it is also important to look at the foundational traditions, especially religious traditions, which have formed us. Those traditions may well offer enduring wisdom that can help us today. For those of us who stand in the Judeo-Christian tradition, the Bible is such a traditional, foundational resource.

In recent years, the Bible (especially the creation narratives in Genesis) has come under criticism for contributing to our ecological woes. In 1967, Lynn White, a cultural historian, blamed Christianity for what has become the environmental crisis. He claimed that the Bible granted a "dominion mandate" that resulted in a kind of human imperialism that ruled at the expense of the rest of the natural world and that Judeo-Christian thought has shown arrogance toward nature.[7]

21

Many of us recall being taught that human beings were told by God to conquer or subdue Earth and have dominion over the fish and the birds and every living thing (Gen 1:26, 28). In years past, this command was illustrated in some books by a diagram of a pyramid divided, from base to top, into mineral creation, vegetation, and animate creation. Humankind appeared at the top. Some of us may well have used that pyramid as teachers. The diagram enforced the understanding that humans stand at the pinnacle of creation and everything below exists to serve humankind.

White's observation provided a "wake-up call" and set wheels in motion. In the last thirty-five or more years, biblical scholars, theologians, and ecologists have responded to White by revisiting biblical texts to re-consider what authors of the texts intended to say about the role of human beings and the status of non-human elements in creation. Through various avenues of contemporary research that make the ancient world more accessible, scholars are re-discovering and examining surprising riches found there regarding issues related to ecological integrity.

Once we begin to re-read the pages of Scripture in an informed manner, we may well be struck with how profoundly the ancients regarded the interrelatedness of all aspects of creation and appreciated creation's intrinsic integrity. For example, we now realize that biblical thought does not generally pose an either/or choice between caring for people and caring for Earth. We discover that the presumed anthropocentric worldview of the Bible has really been imposed by the reader rather than implied by the biblical author. A careful reading of the Bible shows that the principal value of creation as understood by its authors lies less in its usefulness to humans than in the fact that it comes from God and belongs to God.

The biblical view is primarily theocentric and, in turn, cosmocentric. This perspective provides us with grounds for recognizing the dignity of all creation. God is the measure of all things, not humans. The theocentric biblical world picture gives the human being the opportunity to understand self as a member of the community of creation: "These companions of our creaturehood are not only *there*, they are there as things without which I cannot be at all! They surround, support, nourish, delight, allure, challenge and talk back to us."[8]

The Bible, we will discover, is filled with ecological insights that encourage us to live in the midst of creation, care for it, and partner with it. Our focus will be the Hebrew Scriptures.[9] In some detail, we will first consider the Genesis narratives that are foundational to our quest. Other sections of the Hebrew Scriptures will be introduced to "whet appetites" and invite more in-depth study and reflection.

As we move it may prove helpful to keep in mind the image of a "two-level approach" to interpreting the Bible. On the first level, we acknowledge that God enabled human beings to recognize God's revelation and communicate it to others in the course of the history of the Judeo-Christian tradition. In doing so, these human beings, living at different points in history, gave expression to God's revelation using their own language, influenced by their own historical, cultural, social, and scientific outlooks, life experience, level of education, etc.

Once the level of historical conditioning is recognized, we move to a deeper level, the level where we search for the heart of God's revealed, inspired message that endures through every age in spite of human limitation. When we discover this deeper level, we, in turn, find ourselves giving expression to God's revelation through our own language, our historical, cultural, scientific understandings, and experience. This process may sound much simpler than it is. Struggles and debates go on about distinguishing the "two levels." However, those who go about this in the context of believing communities trust that their struggles and efforts to be open to the Spirit's guidance will lead them to some deeper, if still incomplete, grasp of truth. (You are invited to have a Bible nearby and read each scriptural text being discussed. Read aloud, if possible, to experience the dynamism of the Word.)

THE GENESIS CREATION STORIES

As we begin our explorations, the Rev. Michael Dowd, an "itinerant 'Great Story' teller,"[10] helps set the context:

> It was once commonly thought that the history of the Hebrew people was the history of the entire world. We now know, however, that 3,500 years ago, more than 200 years before Moses was born or any part of the Old Testament was written (including the story of Adam and Eve): King Tut III ruled the Egyptian empire's 18th Dynasty; Indo-European charioteers were invading India; China entered the Bronze Age, ruled by the Shang Dynasty; people in southeast Asia were boating to nearby Pacific islands; and vast civilizations could be found in the Americas. All these peoples told inspired and inspiring stories about how the world came into being, how they as a people came into being, and why they were special. To

interpret the early chapters of Genesis or any of the worlds' creation stories as representing the history of the whole world, or to imagine them as competing, rather than complementary, views of reality, is both to miss the symbolic nature of human language and, ironically, to trivialize these sacred texts. A high view of scripture demands that we honor Holy Writ for what it is: a sacred story of how the Hebrew people, inspired by God, imagined their beginnings and their destiny.[11]

As we open the pages of the Hebrew Scriptures, we find not one but two very different creation stories at the beginning of Genesis (1:1-2:4a; 2:4b-25). One of the first steps in approaching these narratives is to determine the ancient literary genre. Confusion on this point leads to much disagreement in interpreting the creation stories.

The creation narratives introduce the first eleven chapters of Genesis, a unit comprised of symbolic stories (some prefer "myths"), which were passed along orally long before they were written down. These stories are symbolic in nature because they grew out of the experience of trying to understand and give expression to realities that are beyond human comprehension, e.g., creation, suffering, etc. The fact that these two creation stories were placed back to back without trying to harmonize them into one story indicates that the compilers appreciated how the unique aspects of each story might speak to us.

Biblical scholar Bruce Birch comments on the value of preserving two creation stories: "We are not required to adjudicate the claims of each to truth. Each communicates its truth within the world it sets up. We are invited into these worlds to receive the disclosure of their truth. To the degree that these stories disclose a reality that rings true to our own experience, their truth can be incorporated into our story. We need not stay in the worlds they create or harmonize their worlds so that they are explainable in terms of our own story of reality."[12]

First Creation Story: Genesis 1:1-2:4a

The first story, the Priestly account, is a powerful, majestic narrative written in the seventh to sixth centuries B.C.E., during the exilic/post-exilic period of Israel's history when it was important to bring order out of the chaotic experience of exile. The drama describes the creation of the cosmos as viewed from Earth and it points to God, the One who creates and delights in the whole of creation. We note that an ancient cosmology is depicted. This is an example of people expressing their theological insights through their current experience and understandings.

In Genesis 1:1-3 we hear: "In the beginning when God created the heavens and the earth, the earth was a formless void and darkness covered the face of the deep, while a wind from God swept over the face of the waters. Then God said: 'Let there be light,' and there was light."[13]

Only God "creates" (*bara'*, in Hebrew). Biblical scholar Richard Lowery notes:

> Outside the Hebrew Bible, *bara'* refers to separating fats from a liquid, skimming cream from milk. As its secondary meaning illustrates, *bara'* well describes God's creative activity in a story that portrays creation as the progressive separating and collecting of primordial waters to allow the solids to appear – sky, earth, and heavenly bodies. The created world is the cream that rises to the top of watery chaos, separated and collected by God. *Bara'* is appropriate for another reason as well. In the biblical world fatness connotes wealth, prosperity, and health. God "creates" a "fat" world, a rich and lavish overflow of goodness, abundant and life-giving at its very core. In this creation story, universal prosperity is simply the way of the world as God called it into being and intends it to be.[14]

In verse 2, Earth is pictured as a formless waste-land, an abyss covered with darkness (*tohu wabohu*). This is the uncontrollable chaos, something empty and wild, without shape or coherence that threatens the social and ecological order of settled life that is agrarian society's worst nightmare. From the per-spective of ancient agrarian peoples, this is the state of the universe when God began creating and "it is also what the universe would return to without God's constant power and care. Creation is the imposition of order on primordial wilderness. The disorder that remains will be pushed to the margins of the zone of life, where it is contained for now, but always threat-ens to violate the boundaries set by God at cre-ation."[15]

THE POWER OF THE WORD

In verse 3, we begin to hear a refrain that will recur throughout: "And God said, 'Let there be....' And it was so." This first creation story is based on the power of the word. In the ancient world, "word" (*dabar*) was not simply a thought that was articu-lated. A word was not fully a word until the utter-ance was effected, that is, what was spoken about happened. Thus, we hear that out of chaos, the form-less void and darkness over the deep, God's spirit-wind (*ruah*) swept over the face of primordial waters and God spoke a word that was fulfilled. Because of

God's creative word, from an empty void comes habitable Earth. God calls and creation responds. In other words, God's word is EVENT.

According to Lowery, God sheds light on dark chaos and sets a boundary between darkness and light to distinguish day and night. He notes that "the universe is introduced to the most fundamental instrument of measure and order in the agrarian world: time. Then God separates the waters of chaos by putting a solid surface in their midst…. In the common ancient Near Eastern view, the sky was thought to be a dome set in place by the gods to hold back the waters of chaos and create a zone of order where life is possible. The created world is a 'biosphere,' 'a bubble of life' suspended in watery chaos, which is kept out from horizon to horizon by the circle of dry land and from above to below by the solid surface of the sky and the firm foundation of the earth."[16]

On the third day (vv. 9-13), God further separates the waters below, causing dry land to appear. The emergence of land allows vegetation to grow. On days four through six (vv. 14-31), God inserts heavenly bodies into the solid surface of the sky and summons into existence swarms of living creatures to swim the seas, to fly between Earth and sky, and to crawl, walk, and feed on the land. Days one to three parallel days four to six in striking symmetical fashion:

Day 1 light, day/night	**Day 4** heavenly lights mark days, nights, seasons
Day 2 sky to separate waters above/below	**Day 5** sky animals water animals
Day 3 dry land appears	**Day 6** land animals/humans

AND GOD SAW THAT IT WAS GOOD

Several times (vv. 4, 10, 12, 18, 21, 25) we hear the deliberate refrain: "And God saw that it was good (*tob*)." In verse 31, when God saw everything that had been made on the sixth day, we hear: "...and indeed, it was very good" (*tob me'od*). That left Israel (and us) in worshipful awareness of God's power and the miracle of the cosmos. God, the cosmic artist, creates a world and blesses it and declares that it is "good."

Creation is both beautiful and in harmony with the divine plan. God creates the world as benevolent not hostile. All aspects of creation are balanced, interrelated, interdependent, harmonious, in right order. Creatureliness *qua* creatureliness is good. Violence is seen as an illegitimate alien intruder into God's good creation. Peace (*shalom*) is primordial.

Biblical scholar Diane Jacobson states, "Genesis 1 tells us right from the beginning that we are merely one part of a vast and wonderful, intricately complex yet

> God, the cosmic artist, creates a world and blesses it and declares that it is "good."

harmonious creation, the whole of which God the Creator pronounces to be 'very good'."[17]

Lowery notes that "*tob* may also imply joy and delight" as well as "intense pleasure at creation's every detail. It is God's cosmic 'Wow!' as each major phase of creation unfolds.... Unrestrained joy, wild delight is a characteristic of creation long before humans are made. The universe is delightful, not because human beings declare it so, but because that is the way God made it."[18] Rev. Scott Hoezee captures God's delight: "In God's supreme attention to detail; in his careful, providential ordering of the earth; and in the happy, exuberant way by which he personally blesses the creatures of this world, we can see clearly the divine delight.... The soaring of the eagle, the breaching of the humpback, the buzzing of the bee, the craning of the giraffe's neck—it all brought joy to God."[19]

In Genesis 1:24-27, we hear that on the same day (the sixth day) that God created the land animals, God created human beings (notice we don't have a day of our own!). The same home is shared by all living beings. Although humans will be given distinct responsibility, they are also one with the other creatures and have something in common with them. "All the createds are relateds."[20]

Genesis 1:27 reports that God created humankind in the divine image, in the image of God they were created, male and female they were created. Much discussion has gone on about the meaning of humans created in the "image" (*selem*) of God. The Hebrew word *selem* elsewhere in Scripture refers to a statue or icon. In the ancient Near Eastern world, the ruler was designated as representative of the gods/goddesses and ruled on their behalf. In turn, images of the ruler were erected to remind governed people of the ruler's power and presence. That presence and power were to be characterized by justice, honor, and the well being of the realm.

In describing the newly created persons as "images" of God, biblical scholar Terence Fretheim observes that the Priestly writer "democratizes this royal image so that all humanity belongs to this sphere and inter-human hierarchical understandings are set aside."[21] The writer may well be saying that humans are to be representatives of God, stewards and caretakers, viceregents, companions, and partners of God in this world. As "images of God" humans, bearing the responsibility to represent God within creation, are to act justly and nobly and compassionately in the place of/on behalf of the Creator. And we humans are morally accountable; blameworthy when we fail, praiseworthy when we do well. Right now the world is off kilter because of how we have exercised our privilege and responsibility, our response-ability.

First Divine Words to Humans Are About Their Relationship to Earth

Tragically, we have in the past read Genesis 1:28 as the divine commandment to conquer every part of creation for human gain with an anti-ecological bias. However, the first divine words to the human beings are about their relationship not to God, but to Earth and all she holds. As representatives of God, humans are to "be fruitful and multiply, and fill the earth, and subdue it; and have dominion over the fish of the sea and over the birds of the air and over every living thing that moves upon the earth," that is, perpetuate life in its fullest and broadest sense.

The command to "subdue" (*kabas*) Earth focuses particularly on cultivation, a difficult task in ancient days. "Subduing" involves development in the created order. This process offers to the human being the task of intra-creational development, bringing the world along to its fullest possible creational potential. God's command passes on to humans the responsibility to act on behalf of creation and to work within the boundaries of our humanness, dealing properly with nature in a way that helps bring forth food and values resources. This has nothing to do with violence, domination, or abusive control.

A study of the verb to have "dominion" (*rada*) indicates that it is associated with royal rule elsewhere in the Hebrew scriptures. As noted above, royal rule, in its ideal exercise, represented God's own rule. Its goal was to ensure the well being and right ordering of the life of God's people (especially the impoverished) and the land and all that it held. God is not commanding benign maintenance and surely not oppressive exploitation but a share in royal, divine rule that can be understood as care-giving and justice-making. As images of God, humans are commissioned to relate to all the rest of creation as God relates to it.

Too often the rule that humans have exercised has been primarily concerned with the way creation can serve human needs and desires, and it has given little thought to creation's own intrinsic value and balance. We have to admit that the devastating crisis of the present moment may be due in significant part to the understanding that gave humans the right to use and abuse creation for the "well being" of more complex forms. But if we accept the biblical

> As images of God, humans are commissioned to relate to all the rest of creation *as God relates to it.*

notion of "dominion," if we share in God's rule, then we must understand God's manner of ruling. It is marked by justice and a loving concern for all of creation.[22]

A significant factor in this creation story so far is that not all agency resides with God. While God is the Creator who fashions the cosmos, God shares creative power: Earth is invited to bring forth vegetation (1:11-12); sun and moon rule the day and the night (1:17-18); waters are to bring forth swarms of living creatures (1:20); Earth is commanded to bring forth animals (1:24); humans are commanded to be fruitful and to have dominion over other creatures (1:28). We see that "God's creative action does not confront that which is created with completely finished facts. The creature's own activity as a constitutive element in the process of creation is seen in harmony with God's action."[23] God empowers creation for its own benefit. Creation is involved in creation!

THE SEVENTH DAY

In the Priestly narrative, creation climaxes and finally coheres in Sabbath rest on the seventh day (2:1-4a). Unfortunately the division of the biblical text into chapters and verses placed the Sabbath at the beginning of chapter 2 of Genesis and separated it from the first six days of creation in chapter 1.

Such a reading tends to set aside the original climax of the seventh day, emphasize work over rest, exalt the creation of humans as the climax of the first creation story, and encourage an anthropocentric reading of the story of creation that has, as we have noted, had destructive consequences in the modern age. The *whole* story requires our attention!

The seventh day differs from other days of creation in form. Each of the previous six days is introduced with the formula "then/and God said" (vv. 3, 6, 9, 14, 20, 24) and ends with the formula "there was evening and there was morning, the first day," and so on (vv. 5, 8, 13, 19, 23, 31). The seventh day narrative breaks the pattern. It opens with an action of God, not a word, and identifies the day in the opening clause not at the end: "And on the seventh day God finished the work… and rested on the seventh day…" (2:2a). Breaking the pattern emphasizes the uniqueness of the Sabbath.

The seventh day is the only day God "blesses" (2:3). Otherwise in this story, only sea creatures, birds, and human beings are "blessed." In these cases, God's blessing is coupled with the admonition to "be fruitful and multiply." Blessing is fundamentally about fertility, long-term well being, and flourishing life. By observing the blessed Sabbath, the world expresses gratitude to the God who calls us to live such a blessed life. God also makes the Sabbath day "holy." Holiness has to do with the state of persons or things set apart from normal use or activity to ensure ritual purity. The seventh day is set apart from the other six days and becomes a special day indeed.

In Maria Harris' inspiring work, *Proclaim Jubilee: A Spirituality for the Twenty-First Century*, she raises the questions: "What does it mean to live by Sabbath and as Sabbath? What does it mean to keep Sabbath?"[24] In reflecting on these questions, Maria Harris says that Sabbath means we practice *shavat* or cessation. Israel is to rest because God rested. God "is not a workaholic; Yahweh has no need to be more secure, more sufficient, more in control, or more noticed."[25] Nor do we. God's world is not a place of endless productivity, ambition, or anxiety.

> The Sabbath promise concerns not only restoration of human life but also restoration of all creation. The challenge of keeping Sabbath is *the challenge of living in a new way....*

Sabbath is not measured by what is accomplished, but by what is inspired and envisioned when we take time to practice *shavat*. Sabbath was never entirely ceremonial. Instead, from early in its promulgation, Sabbath included the regular practice of justice. It involved ethical and moral teaching about human beings' relations with other humans (spouse, children, enslaved and indentured workers, strangers), as well as concern for animals and the land. Sabbath observance allowed the land to rest, enabling it to collect its energies. During the Sabbath year the fields, vineyards, and olive trees were to lie fallow and anything that they produced was to be left for the poor, slaves, tenants, the livestock and wild animals (Exod 23:10-11; Lev 25:1-7). Everyone, including the animals, had a right to enjoy the fruits of the land at rest.

The understanding that Earth and all it holds belong to God undergirded Sabbath observance. This reflection has been offered by Rabbi Marc Tannenbaum:

> God said, "The relation between yourselves and me is always that of strangers and settlers. If you will live in the world like strangers, remembering that you are here but temporarily, then I will be a settler in your midst in that my Presence (the *Shechinah*) will dwell with you permanently. But if you will regard yourselves as settlers, as permanent owners of the land on which you live, when the land is actually not yours but mine, my Presence will be a stranger in that it will not dwell in your midst. In any case, you, O Israel, you and I cannot be strangers and settlers at the same time. If you act the stranger, I will be the

settler, and if you act the settler, I must be the stranger," said God.[26]

The Sabbath promise concerns not only restoration of human life but also restoration of all creation. The challenge of keeping Sabbath is the challenge of living in a new way so that God's plan for creation is more evident here and now. Through Sabbath observance the world can be reconsecrated despite the ravages of sin that have disfigured it.

SECOND CREATION STORY: GENESIS 2:4B-25

In the second creation story, the Yahwist account (*ca.* tenth century B.C.E.) begins on a barren stretch of soil with a stream welling up out of Earth and watering the ground. The Creator, a more rural and homey figure than the cosmic God of the first story, fashions the first human from Earth and this relationship is captured in a play on words, 'adam (human being) from 'adamah (Earth). Various English translations have been proposed to capture this linguistic and philosophical connection, such as "earthling" from "Earth," or "human" from "humus." 'Adam is forever linked to the other creatures who are formed from the 'adamah. God then breathes into the nostrils of 'adam the breath of life (2:7).

In Genesis 2:5, we hear that the Lord God had not caused it to rain upon Earth, and there was no one to cultivate/serve (*'abad*) the ground. However, in Genesis 2:15, God took *'adam* and settled this human in the garden of Eden to "cultivate/serve" (*'abad*) and "take care of/protect/keep" (*samar*) the garden. It is striking to note that *'adam* is told to "serve" the garden. Here is an image of a human being as a member of creation engaged in its "service," so to speak.

"Take care of/protect/keep" (*samar*) is the same Hebrew verb used in the great Aaronic blessing in Num 6:24: "The Lord bless you and *keep* you." Also the verb appears in Ps 121:7-8: "The Lord will *keep* you from all evil; he will *keep* your life. The Lord will *keep* your going out and coming in from this time on and forevermore." If God's keeping of us means God's careful, attentive, protective guarding of all that we are and all that we have, then our keeping of God's world should mean the same. We will keep, guard, watch over, attend to, caretake, and protect all that is God's, all that is gift from God. The "humbler" image of the human who is made from *'adamah* as are other creatures and is called to serve and keep the garden helps to put the notion of "dominion" into proper perspective.

Once God has fashioned the human being from Earth and breathed the divine breath into the human, God announces that it is not good for the human being to be alone (Gen 2:18). Theologians Michael Himes and Kenneth Himes point out that

41

there is insistence here that humans are to be in relationship and that companionship is the ground for the creation of the sexes. But it is striking to note that human beings

> The "humbler" image of the human who is made from 'adamah as are other creatures and is called to serve and keep the garden helps to put the notion of "dominion" into proper perspective.

are not intended to be in relationship solely with one another. This intention for relationship is also the reason for the creation of the various kinds of wild animals and birds of the air (2:19). The natural world is not only intended to be cared for by humans—it is intended for companionship with human beings. Companionship implies mutuality. It excludes the reduction of either side (especially the non-human side) of the relationship to tool or object.[27]

BEING OF THE SOIL

Professor of the Hebrew Bible Theodore Hiebert explains that when one recognizes that throughout the epic, the Yahwist author consistently uses the term 'adamah for arable soil in particular, one realizes that there is an even more precise claim about human life being made here. It is the claim that humanity's archetypal agricultural vocation is implanted within humans by the very stuff out of which they are made, the arable soil itself. Humans, made from farmland, are destined to farm it in life and to return to it in death (3:19, 23).

Such a sense is natural in a subsistence economy in which the outcomes of each growing season can mean life or death. But it is not so natural in a highly specialized modern culture in which our dependence on the environment has been largely obscured by our technology. Nor is it so natural in our Western idealistic theological tradition, which has taught us to divide the spiritual from the material. Yet it is a sense we will have to recover in some new way, as our best instincts, our best scientists, our best theologians all tell us, if we are to survive this ecological crisis. We will have to recover this sense of interrelatedness in terms of the modern scientific, social, and intellectual world, which is our reality. Part of this endeavor is reconnecting our theological reflection with the roots of such a perspective in our scriptural tradition.[28]

AN EXCURSUS: CONTEMPORARY MODELS OF THE "DOMINION" IMAGE

The discussion of the creation stories gives rise to the consideration of contemporary implications of the "dominion" image. How we understand this image is key to how we relate to creation. Today some would say that even redefined notions of "dominion" are dangerous in so far as they remain anthropocentric. It may be helpful to take a look at how several contemporary writers/theologians are wrestling with the dominion image.

1. Elizabeth Johnson suggests that at least three models can be considered in regard to how we image our relationship to Earth/creation: models of kingship, stewardship, and kinship.

The kingship model is based on hierarchical dualism that sees humanity separated from Earth and placed in a position of absolute dominion over all other creatures who are made for us. In this view the creatures of the world are ranked according to their participation in the fullness of the spirit, with greater value assigned to those higher up on the great chain of being. At the lowest level is inorganic matter; next comes vegetative matter, followed by animals, human beings and non-physical spirits or angels. In the progression from the pebble to the poodle to the person, with women somewhere between the latter two, the higher order of creatures has the right to use and control the lower. This is the patriarchal pyramid resulting in top-down domination of nature by humans.

The stewardship model keeps the structure of hierarchical dualism but calls for human beings to be responsible caretakers or guardians of Earth and all its creatures. Having neither fur nor feathers, human beings need to use Earth creatively for shelter, food, and the basics of survival, developing culture as the medium through which these achievements are passed on. But in so doing, they know that they must care for Earth, even in terms of their own self-interest. In this model, humanity is still at the top of the pyramid of being but has the duty to protect and preserve what seems weaker and more vulnerable. This position is clearly an improvement over the absolute ruler model, for it guarantees a modicum of respectful use of Earth. Particularly in the political and legal spheres, its vision is highly beneficial for crafting policy. Yet it misses the crucial aspect of human dependence upon that which we steward. Upon reflection, the stewardship model itself finds its deepest foundation in the kinship model that traces an organic connection between human beings and Earth.

If separation is not the ideal but connection is; if dualism is not the ideal but the relational embrace of diversity is; if hierarchy is not the ideal but mutuality is, then **the kinship model** more closely approximates reality. It sees humans and Earth with all its creatures intrinsically related as companions in a community of life. Because we are all mutually interconnected, the flourishing or damaging of one ultimately affects all. This kinship attitude does not measure differences on a scale of higher or lower ontological dignity but appreciates them as integral elements in the robust thriving of the whole. Articulated within a religious perspective, the kinship stance knows that we humans are interrelated parts and products of a world that is continually being made and nurtured by the Creator Spirit. Its attitude is one of respect for Earth and all living creatures including ourselves as manifestations of the Spirit's creative energy; its actions cooperate with the Spirit in helping it flourish. What goes on in this instance is neither a sentimental love of nature nor an ignorance that levels all distinctions between human beings and other forms of life. Rather what is involved is a recognition of the truth: human existence is in fact one with the immensity of all that is.[29]

2. Brennan Hill discusses the "**partnership model**" and the ethic of companionship. This model requires a change from seeing ourselves as being at the center of things. Human needs and considerations have to be put side by side with the needs of other creatures. This does not imply that humans are not unique, free, and bound by singular responsibilities. It does, however, call for a broader field of consideration in making decisions that will affect many levels of nature. It might even call for sacrifice on our part at times when our development and growth will affect the lives of other beings. The partnership model takes into consideration the needs of creatures

other than humans. It develops a respect for Earth and for other living things to a point where all are given serious consideration in every decision that is made for progress and development. This model entails working with nature rather than trying to conquer it.[30]

3. Mary Elizabeth Moore acknowledges that some have a problem with the model of stewardship, thinking that it still points to domination and superiority. Others think that this model is an answer representing a humble respect and care-giving role for God's creation. One aspect that is often neglected is **stewardship with the rest of creation**. Such stewardship grows from compassion, from feeling with the creatures of Earth. A sense of interconnection and responsibility is combined with ability to feel with Earth. When stewardship theories focus only on human responsibility *to* God and creation, and *for* the care of creation, the idea remains human-centered. What is lost is the compassionate relationship and responsibility of *every* part of creation with the whole. Stewardship has to do with tending and caring in mutual relationship *with* Earth. Every part of creation has a role to play. Humans are stewards *with* the soil and sky, as the plants and animals are stewards with us.[31]

4. Michael Himes and Kenneth Himes, dealing with the elements of a new ethic to address the ecological crisis, discuss the **companionship motif** found in the second creation story:

> Governed by images of stewardship and ruled by precepts based on self interest, our moral imaginations are unable to envision an environmental ethic that is adequate to the Jewish and Christian heritage. In contrast, images of companionship encourage the moral imagination to consider that more than the good of the individual self is at stake. Once the intrinsic good of creation is seen, then approaches to the environmental crisis that treat creation only as an instrumental good for humanity become inadequate.... Rediscovering the "thou" dimension of all creation provides a corrective to the tendency to relate to nature only as "it" by moving beyond the technological vision of instrumental rationality to a reawakened sacramental vision of companionship. So fundamental a reorientation alters the context for assessing our responsibility toward the environment.[32]

Unfortunately, by the time we reach Genesis 3, human sin and alienation appear, leading to broken relationships. Sin continues to escalate through the primeval history (Gen1-11) as humans do violence to the order of God's creation and fail to honor the boundaries of their humanness. As a result, all creation suffers!

THE FLOOD ACCOUNTS: GENESIS 6-9

As broken relationships increase, a striking crisis point is reached in the flood accounts. In response to the widespread violence that had infected Earth, the narrator describes the inner divine reaction stunningly (6:5-8). God sees how great the wickedness of human sin on Earth has become and God regrets that humans have been created. The divine heart is grieved! In response, God declares that humans and all animals will be wiped out. Divine consternation and disappointment are obvious since God's vision for what the world might have been has been dashed by narrow and self-centered human sinfulness. But a ray of hope appears when we are told that Noah found favor in the sight of God (6:8). The divine judgmental decision is moderated as God decides not to let the rebellion of humankind sway the divine intention for creation. A second chance is granted.

Noah will do as God commands, that is, accept creatureliness, and let God be God.

The story weaves together various source strands. Attention is given to the boarding of the ark, lists of people and animals and birds that are saved, and to the chronology of the flood event. We hear throughout echoes of the first creation stories. God opens the windows of heaven and the fountains of the great deep (7:11). The separation of dry land and sea, so necessary for the well being of living things, collapses in this resurgence of primal watery chaos. With chaos threatening to overwhelm, with the deep abyss ready to engulf the ark, God remembers the inhabitants of the "floating species preserve."[33]

As in the first creation story (1:2), God's Spirit blows over the chaotic waters and the waters subside. Chaos is controlled once again and *shalom* is restored. The human family and the animals move through this horrendous experience sustained by the divine promise that ensures a future relationship with God for all creation. God saves a precious remnant of humans and animals in the ark, the fragile ship of life and personally gives the directive for everyone to leave the ark. Representatives of everything that moves on Earth go out of the ark by families (8:17-19) so that they may be fruitful and abound on Earth. "Divine graciousness," notes theologian William French, "is seen in this first species-protection project."[34]

God's promises focus on agricultural life, climate, seasons, and the daily rhythm: "As long as the earth endures, seedtime and harvest, cold and heat, summer and winter, day and night, shall not cease" (8:22). Come what may, God promises that the rhythm of the natural order, disrupted by the flood, will continue and remain steady and regular.

In Genesis 9:1-17, God makes provisions to safeguard creation by blessing Noah and his family and giving the command: "Be fruitful and multiply, and fill the earth" (9:1). Note that this time God does not include the directive to "subdue" and "have dominion." Perhaps, suggests theologian Steven Bouma-Prediger, "God thought better of giving that command this time, given the mess humans had made of the earth. Taking the command to rule in their own hands, mistaking dominion for domination, the human earth-creature had perverted its royal responsibility and polluted the earth."[35]

While creation is renewed, however, gone is the perfect peace and harmony of Eden. Ominously, God tells Noah and his family that "the fear and dread of you shall rest on every animal of the earth, and on every bird of the air, on everything that creeps on the ground, and on all the fish of the sea; into your hands they are delivered" (9:2). Human history after the fall and flood is marked both by new blessing and also by painful recognition that human life is now sustained through the slaughter of animals, birds, and fish who recoil in fright. Whereas before God gave animals and humans only green plants for food (1:29-30), now a boundary has been crossed, and God says to humans that "every moving thing that lives shall be food for you" (9:3). Historically this condition of the eating of animals may well have been a concession by the Hebrew authors in their time to the need for food in a famine-ridden world.

Still no blood that bears the principle of life may be eaten (9:4). Life belongs to God and should be returned to its source. Killing animals is to be taken seriously, for God is source of their life. Though humans are now carnivores, respect for life is still the rule. It is striking that God puts so much stock in the saving of animals; indeed, God's remembrance of animals belongs to the same initiative as God's remembering Noah. Concern for the life of animals leads into a concern for human life (vv. 5-6). And here we are assured once again that humans con-tinue to be made in the "image" of God (v. 6). The implication is that even though animals are given into human hands, humans made in God's image are not given a license for exploitation nor a diminution in the task of dominion. Unfortunately, the reality of fear makes relationships with the animal world

> God's remembrance of animals belongs to the same initiative as God's remembering Noah.

much more difficult and complex. We will see that the prophets in portraying the end-time show the return of harmony to relationships between humans and animals (*e.g.*, Isa 11:6-9).

And now we hear the sweeping, all-inclusive, divinely initiated covenant:

> As for me, I am establishing my covenant with you and your descendants after you, and with *every living creature* that is with you, the birds, the domestic animals, and every animal of the earth with you, as many as came out of the ark. I establish my covenant with you, that never again shall *all flesh* be cut off by the waters of a flood.... This is the sign of the covenant that I make between me and you and *every living creature* that is with you for all future generations; I have set my bow in the clouds, and it shall be a sign of the covenant *between me and the earth...between me and you and every living creature of all flesh*....When the bow is in the clouds, I will see it and remember the everlasting covenant *between God and every living creature of all flesh that is on the earth*" (9:8-16; emphasis added).

The covenant established by God is not made with Noah alone but with Earth and her plethora of creatures, the *whole of creation*. Notice the repetitious wording in Gen 9:8-16. It is as if the speaker (God) is trying to phrase this contract in the most sweeping way possible so that no living being of any kind will be left out. This is God's inclusive covenant with *all living beings* and *Earth*, that is, the entire created order. God is obligated unilaterally and unconditionally as the covenant is established in love and upheld in eternal faithfulness. This covenant will never need to be renewed; it stands forever, regardless of what people do. God will relate to creation with unlimited patience and forbearance; the divine commitment for a harmonious creation is intensified.

The sign of the covenant, the rainbow, is a reminder for God not humans. In earlier Mesopotamian myths, the bow was probably symbol of the arched weapon of the divine warrior who was victorious over the chaotic waters. Hanging the bow in the sky was the sign that the primeval war was over, chaos was conquered, and the created world could rest secure from threatening forces. God sets the bow in the clouds as an indication that never again will God be provoked to use a weapon, no matter how provocative human beings become. The last word is spoken by the one who re-creates: "I will remember my covenant."

William French observes that by paying close attention to previously neglected details and biblical texts, a growing circle of scholars is recovering the centrality of God's ecological covenant with Earth. Instead of concentrating on humans as the apex of creation and the mandate given to them to have dominion, these scholars situate the opening texts of Genesis within the broader frame of events including creation, humanity's fall into sin, the flood, the new blessing, and God's covenant with Earth. Understanding Genesis 1-9 as a unit, we discover that the buildup does not end with the creation of humans but moves from creation of plants, animals, humans to a covenant with the entire community of Earth. God's covenant with all creation is more fundamental than God's particular covenants with humanity or with Israel. The flood accounts close on a distinctively biocentric note!

Humanity's unique capacities of rationality may serve to warrant our "dominion" over Earth, but a broader ecological reading of Genesis suggests that humanity is also distinguished by our capacities to reject God's command, to fall into sin, and thereby to

> A growing circle of scholars is recovering the *centrality* of God's ecological covenant with Earth.

unleash violence into the world. French notes that "human 'dominion' is more about responsible ecological stewardship of the planet—our common ark in space—than simply a grant of unlimited rights in the use of nonhuman living things."[36]

Considering the contemporary situation, French puts before us some challenging questions:

> Is not humanity today unleashing a new "flood" upon Earth, one whose waves threaten to destroy significant parts of the divinely created global ecosystem, and to endanger life dependent upon the well-being of the entire community of creation?... The currents of this "eco-deluge" while processive and building gradually and quietly, are inexorable in their tidal flow and force. The destruction emerging from countless individual, corporate, and governmental decisions and policies mounts steadily higher and higher.... And given the increasing rates of ecosystem destruction, jungle clearing, and species extinction, who can be surprised that "fear and dread" of the human juggernaut rests on every nonhuman living species?... When we break the ecosystem structures, established climatic patterns, and biospheric balances, what will keep the chaotic

forces at bay?… If we insist on violating the natural constraints formed into the very fabric of creation, will we not see a desolation of land, its marvelous species, and its peoples?... Divine covenants both empower freedoms and sets constraints.[37]

THEOLOGICAL UNDERPINNINGS IN THE GENESIS NARRATIVES

At this point, let us pause and identify some of the theological insights that begin to surface through a careful reading of the foundational narratives in Genesis:

• God, with unconditional love, is the ultimate source of the creative process.

• While the God of the first creation story (Gen 1:1-2:4a) may appear to stand apart from creation as transcendent, the God of the second story (2:4b-25) is an immanent God, an intimate God, if you will, forming the first human and the animals from the earth (the potter and clay image), breathing the breath of life into the human person (2:7).

• What emerges in the course of God's creative activity belongs to God.

• The entire creation begins as a harmonious community.

• All is created "good."

• Humans are made of precisely the same "stuff," *'adamah*, as every other created being; humanity is not over or against nature but part of it.

• As "images of God," humans bear the responsibility to help maintain justice (right relationships) and *shalom* (well being) and prevent the tearing of the web of relationships.

• Humans are given responsibility not simply for maintenance but for development, that is, bringing creation along to its fullest possible potential. A dynamic situation is created in which the future lies open to various possibilities.[38]

• In considering the Genesis stories, we may well find ourselves moving beyond the model of "stewardship" and on to concepts that express the mutual relationship of all parts of creation, such as community, partnership, kinship, and companionship.

• The understanding of the Sabbath as part of the first creation story forms the basis later in Torah not only for liturgical observance but also for the demands of just living that include right relationship between God, humankind, and the Earth/land.

• The Genesis flood stories are connected to the earlier creation accounts in Genesis. If we consider Genesis 1-9 as a unit, we see the pattern of creation, destruction/dis-integration, new creation emerging. This suggests that creation is not a one time event but is ongoing. This pattern will surface throughout the Bible and climax at the end of the book of Revelation with the marvelous vision of the new heaven and the new Earth and God's words: "See, I am making all things new" (21:5).

The Genesis texts are rich indeed in providing ecological wisdom. In the past many of us have been taught that the watershed event of the Hebrew Scriptures was the Exodus/Sinai account. Surely God's saving, liberating intervention in Israel's history was of great consequence for the emergence of the covenant people. However, in emphasizing the Exodus, we backed into the creation stories and saw them as a prologue to the "essential" story of the liberation of oppressed humans. We now see that the creation narratives do not function simply as a prologue but rather they are foundational stories, encompassing all creation.

We now turn to other parts of the Hebrew Bible to see what is said on the topic of ecology. Consider this a sampling of the fare offered in the wisdom tradition, the psalms, and the prophetic books. Hopefully, "appetites will be whetted" to engage in further study and reflection.

> We now see that the creation narratives do not function simply as a prologue but rather they are *foundational* stories, encompassing *all* creation.

THE WISDOM TRADITION

Another important section of Scripture that provides a glimpse of Israel's perspective on creation is the Wisdom tradition. Biblical scholar Diane Jacobson offers several helpful observations about Wisdom literature:

1) One can define wisdom as being a movement in ancient Israel, indeed in the entire Ancient Near East, which deals, on the one hand, with everyday life and how to get along in it—how to cope—and, on the other hand, with speculation about how the world works and why.
2) One can perhaps best explain wisdom as being a certain attitude toward the world or a certain quest. The attitude is that the world makes sense. The quest is twofold: to discover the sense of the world, and to order one's life in compliance with this sense.

3) Wisdom is that part of the biblical tradition which does not start with revelation and tradition; rather wisdom starts with observation of the world and with the conviction that truth can be learned, attained by such observation.

4) For our purposes, one of the most significant facts about the wisdom tradition is that wisdom is rooted in the notion that God created the world, and for this reason, the world has some sense, some order to it.[39]

In this section on Wisdom literature, we will consider what Woman Wisdom says to us about her and our relation to nature and creation. Then we will take a look at the book of Job.

BOOK OF PROVERBS (8:22-36; SEE ALSO WISDOM 7)

In Proverbs 8, we encounter the Woman Wisdom (*hokmah* in Hebrew; *sophia* in Greek) who speaks (preaches!) about who she is and what she brings to human beings by way of instruction and guidance. Notice that embedded in the heart of this chapter (8:22-36), we hear that Woman Wisdom was created at the beginning and was present as all things were ordered: "Ages ago I was set up; at the first, before the beginning of the earth" (8:23).

Professor of Religion and Theology Raymond C. Van Leeuwen notes that Wisdom appears to have been created by God, but she exists prior to and on a different plane from all other creatures. Wisdom is connected with the whole process of creation as the prior condition for the existence and functioning of all things (in Wisdom 8:6, Woman Wisdom is presented as the fashioner of the cosmos). She belongs both to God and creation. Wisdom is completely wise since she has seen it all from the beginning. The description of God's cosmic acts of creating and establishing suggests that all of creation is within her purview.

Wisdom then is concerned not only about human beings. She also knows the basic structures, patterns, and functions of all of creation. Israel understood that the order of divine creation set limits and determined the norms for human activity. According to the Wisdom tradition, human culture and society are embedded in the matrix of the world God made. This matrix was designed to keep humans from evil and foster goodness. Human order is grounded in cosmic order.[40]

The text moves from cosmic construction to joy and delight (Prov 8:30-31; Wisdom is personified as a "craftsperson" or a "little child" rejoicing in the creation of the cosmos). Feasting follows (9:1-6)! Here is reflected an ancient pattern that combines joy in building with celebration at its completion. In all of this, Woman Wisdom is the delight of God!

"In Proverbs 8, Woman Wisdom who was present at creation and is intimately linked with the continuing order of creation calls to humanity and invites us to live our lives, both individually and societally, in accordance with the cosmic harmony and divine intention of creation," observes Jacobson.[41] At the heart of creativity in biblical Wisdom texts, Woman Wisdom provides a corrective to the dualistic and dominating conceptions of the relationship between the divine and creation. She, who is deeply present within nature as God's creation, invites us to discover ourselves within rather than apart from our complex global ecosystem. Wisdom invites contemplation of creation!

A lovely and encouraging piece of advice is given by Dominican theologian Mary Catherine Hilkert, O.P. in her discussion of what the figure of Wisdom has to say to preachers. In Proverbs 31:25 where Wisdom "laughs at the time to come," the author asks:

> What does all this say about the life of all women and men who would be friends of Wisdom? What about the life of a preacher

or a community of preachers? On the one hand, we are involved in the most basic refashioning of society and the earth, but, on the other hand, true wisdom means we won't take ourselves too seriously. It is God's grace that ultimately changes hearts, not our words or even our lives. Among the many ways we preach is through a spirit of festivity and celebration, delighting in God's creation and in the midst of very serious questions about our own future and the future of the earth, having the freedom to "laugh at the days to come."[42]

BOOK OF JOB (38:1-42:6)

Job, a righteous man who found himself in the depths of suffering, struggled with the question: why me? Job's friends defended God and suggested that Job consider how he was unrighteous and merited this suffering. According to them, disaster was understood as a moral discipline, a punishment. Job maintained his innocence and called on God to get some things straight. He rejected his friends' conclusions and embraced an alternative paradigm that allowed him to declare the disasters unmerited. He looked for someone to blame and that "someone" was God. From Job's perspective, God was unfair and unjust. In the end, only God could settle things.

One might read this book and conclude that God never did answer Job's questions about the reasons for his suffering. Rather, at the end (42:1-6), God emphasized to Job that God is God and creatures are just going to have to be satisfied humbly with being creatures, especially when they do not understand God's ways. However, re-readings of this wonderful book can lead one to conclude that God did, in fact, provide answers to Job's questions and the answers are found in the heart of creation itself (38:1-42:6). God, who had been silent since the prologue, finally broke the cosmic silence and began speaking out of a whirlwind (38:1) in some of the most magnificent poetry the Hebrew Scriptures have to offer us.

God is cast as the "wisdom teacher" who tests Job's comprehension of his place in the universe. The encounter between God and Job occurs in the midst of the natural world. Out of the whirlwind, God challenges: "Who is this that darkens counsel by words without knowledge?" (38:2). Job is challenged as one whose words presume knowledge and status that he does not possess. He is ordered to stand before God and engage in the hearing with God that Job himself has demanded. And God begins speaking in wonderful cosmic descriptions of creation. This is hardly what Job was expecting!

The first part of the divine response (chaps. 38-39) concerns itself with cosmology and meteorology: the structure of Earth, control of the sea, function of the dawn, abysses, dwellings of light and darkness, storehouses of snow, hail, lightning, and wind, the course of rain for the desert, the origin of dew, rain, ice, and frost, movement of constellations, control of clouds and rain. Following meteorological and cosmological descriptions comes attention to five pairs of animals: lions and ravens; mountain goats and deer; onager and wild ox; ostrich and war horse; hawk and vulture. God's descriptions are striking indeed.

When God refers to the structures and workings of the world and describes animal behaviors, there is a kind of pride and a sensitivity that bespeaks satisfaction and protective concern. This is the Creator who alone understands and manages the entire sweep of creation, who invites Job to contemplate its resplendence and complexity to the extent that he is able. God asks questions about nature and Job gains insight about human limitation. Professor of Old Testament Dianne Bergant observes: "The artistry of God can be seen in the splendor of the universe; God's wisdom in its delicate balance; God's imagination in its diversity; God's providence in its inherent fruitfulness…. It is not enough to say that creation is the medium through which God is revealed; in a very real sense, the medium is itself the revelation."[43]

Job is invited to see all of creation as part of God's design. And the striking realization is that God is describing a world that exists long before humans appear and has its own intrinsic worth. With no humans around, God brings rain on "a land where no one lives, on the desert, which is empty of human life; to satisfy the waste and desolate land, and to make the ground put forth grass" (38:26-27). The scale of this creation is so vast and wondrous and important to God that humans are small indeed in the large picture. (Science now tells us that it rained for millions of years on early Earth—long before humans appeared!)[44]

JOB AWAKENS TO HIS LIMITED HUMAN PLACE IN GOD'S CREATION

Job finally realizes that he has dealt with things too wonderful for him to understand (42:3) and he humbly acknowledges his error. Job is righteous but he is mistaken. He now views life not from an uncritical anthropocentric point of view but rather from the stance that allows him to acknowledge the divine, cosmic scope of creation and his limited human place in the very large plan of God. We discover then that God's concentration on the wonders of creation is not an avoidance of the issues of human life, but rather, it is a response. Job was challenged to give up his treasured place "in the center" or "on top" and see creation from God's viewpoint. Job's demands make sense only in the context of a paradigm that is limited and anthropocentric in nature. God presents a paradigm that is cosmocentric! This "paradigm shift" has challenging implications for human beings.

Dianne Bergant notes that God is revealed to Job as the source of mind-boggling creativity, not as an arbiter preoccupied only with human affairs. God shows that divine artistry and protection have been lavished on all creation, not only on human beings. Job begins to see that human history unfolds within the broader context of the natural world and not vice versa.

> The God whom Job now knows is the mysterious power who brought forth the world and who is somehow revealed in and through that world. This God can provide for the entire resplendent universe without being distracted from the specific needs of fragile human beings, because God's designs are grander than, but do include, human history. God has taken suffering, the most pressing concern of human history,

and has situated it within a broader context, that of material creation in its entirety. There, in the midst of measureless natural grandeur, the ambiguity of human life can be confronted with the honesty and humility that it requires, an honesty and humility that can admit to and accept the limited capacity of human comprehension. Creation itself has expanded Job's vision and called him to a deepening faith that goes beyond understanding.[45]

In reflecting on the profound human struggle between anthropology and cosmology, Bergant says that this struggle "pits the search for understanding against the enormity of the universe in such a way that the human spirit is enraptured not broken…. In the end, cosmology does not defeat anthropology; it opens its arms to welcome back the prodigal child."[46] We learn that we are part of the whole. In Aldo Leopold's words, we are "plain member and citizen" of the land community.[47]

Like Job we may want answers to our human problems, but the questions we ask may come out of a flawed anthropocentric paradigm. We may challenge God on human, moral issues as we understand them, but we learn from Job that the divine speeches require a prolonged and disciplined act of contemplation as the first task. We need to be silent and contemplate. Biblical scholar Carol Newsom notes that "there are probably not many ethics courses in colleges or seminaries that spend the first three days in silence—one day in the forest, one day at the shore of the sea, one night in a field gazing at the stars."

Newsom goes on to say:

> Yet something like that is what God requires of Job as the starting point for a new moral understanding. The moral sense of nature is above all an affirmation that the natural world has intrinsic value. The morning stars' cry of joy (38:7) is the recognition of the intrinsic value that God speaks of as "goodness" in Genesis 1. The starting point for the development of the moral sense in the divine speeches is a contemplation of the goodness of the natural world: earth and rain and raven…. The divine speeches do not primarily serve to lay out a moral teaching about the world. They serve, rather, as a revelatory experience. Such moments of revelation always have an elusive, enigmatic quality that escapes reduction to a "message"….They contain the generative seed of a wholly new way of understanding God, the world, and oneself. Teasing out the possibilities of such a

moment may require a lifetime, but in that process one engages the existential questions of identity and vocation that God poses to each person.[48]

A WORLD WIDE AND WILD ENOUGH TO ABSORB HUMAN SUFFERING

Before we leave Job, let us return to the question of human suffering and its relation to creation. Again Newsom offers words of enlightenment when she says that confronting the reality of the presence of the chaotic in the design of the world is essential (represented by Behemoth and Leviathan in chaps. 40-41), but if the divine speeches had nothing to say to Job except that pain is part of life, then they would hardly be worth reading. One has to ask how they comfort and strengthen. It is essential to remember that Leviathan is not the only topic in the divine speeches. Before God speaks of that emblem of the chaotic, God has already described a world in which the chaotic, although present, is contained within secure boundaries of a created order that is also rich with goodness.

The first divine speech (38-39) acknowledges Job's sense of a fall into the abyss. With its orderly pattern of visually powerful images, the divine speech is a verbal re-creation of the world. Hearing the words of the establishment of Earth on secure foundations, the reliable return of the dawn each day, the regulation of life-giving water, and the nurture of animals is a reassurance that in spite of the reality of pain and loss, God's creation supports and sustains.

The divine speeches offer comfort in another way, too. A person who has suffered a great loss or who has finally faced up to a painful reality long denied often experiences an overwhelming sense of isolation, alienation, and godforsakenness. There is a need to share the burden, and yet such sharing can be difficult. The speeches address this issue by means of the creation imagery they employ.[49] Bouma-Prediger observes that "God's whirlwind speeches forcibly remind Job not only of God's power but also of the expanse and mystery of the created world—a world not of human making. Such a world, beyond human control or knowledge, is able somehow to absorb the weight of human sorrow.... When God is at the center, and the human thereby displaced, there is a world wide and wild enough to absorb the pain of human suffering."[50] Speaking of the relation of the created world to issues of pain and grief, Czech philosopher E. Kohak reflects on the book of Job:

> [A] human alone ... cannot bear the pain.
> [A human] can do that only when the grief
> can disperse, radiate out and be absorbed.

[Even] fellow humans and their work, bearing the same burden, cannot absorb it.... To reconcile, that is what the forest does, silent and accepting, as if God were present therein, taking the grief unto [God's self]. When humans no longer think themselves alone, masters of all they survey, when they discern the humility of their place in the vastness of God's creation, then that creation and its God can share the pain.... That is the age-old wisdom of the book of Job.... When God speaks ... [God] speaks not of pain but of the vastness of the creation, of the gazelle in her mountain fastness, the mighty creatures of the deep sea. God is not avoiding the issue. [God] is teaching Job the wisdom of bearing the pain that can neither be avoided nor abolished but can be shared when there is a whole living creation to absorb it.... When the human, in the solitude of dusk, surrenders ... pride of place and learns to bear the shared pain, [the human] can begin to understand the pain that cannot be avoided as a gift which teaches compassion and opens understanding.... [51]

THE PSALMS

Recommended for reflection: Psalms 8, 19, 24, 65, 104, 148

When we enter the psalter, we listen to and are invited to join with Israel in prayer. Israel broke forth in songs of praise when the wonder of God's creation was contemplated. As we read the psalms that refer to creation, it is clear that Israel understood that everything made gives evidence of God's sovereign, benevolent rule and that Earth and all she holds belong to Yahweh (Ps 24:1). Reflection on Psalm 104 reveals how Israel understood her relation to God and creation.

PSALM 104

Those who pray this beautiful song of creation are truly aware of the blessings and "goodness" of all that God has created. The *inclusio* that begins and ends this psalm, "Bless the Lord, O my soul," leaves no doubt that creation is God's work and gift. The interdependence of all elements of creation is marvelous to behold and we note that humans are among many creatures that depend on God for life; they are part of the weave.

We are drawn to celebrate God's creation of the world (vv. 2-9), the gift of water which is not a threat here but sustainer of life; plants for animals and humans; the trees that God waters (vv 10-16); the presence of birds and wild animals; the creation and role of the moon, sun, and sea and all that live on Earth and in the sea (vv. 19-26). This Creator God sets up the world and continues to care for and sustain it. As one moves through the psalm, the interconnection of the various aspects of creation is evident and celebrated. One part of creation cares for another: springs gush forth and provide water for living beings; Earth yields growth that provides food and safe places for animals and humans; mountains offer refuge; heavenly bodies regulate the cycles and rhythms of life.

All creatures depend on God as they "all look to you to give them their food in due season; when you give to them, they gather it up; when you open your hand, they are filled with good things" (vv. 27-28). God is responsible for the breath of life: "When you hide your face, they are dismayed; when you take away their breath, they die and return to their dust. When you send forth your spirit, they are created; and you renew the face of the ground" (vv. 29-30). The vocabulary—breath/spirit, dust, created, ground—

recalls Genesis 1-2. The only appropriate response is that of wonder, praise, and gratitude: "I will sing to the Lord as long as I live; I will sing praise to my God while I have being" (v. 33). Everything is "good, very, very good." However, if evil appears, God will remove it from the face of Earth (v. 35). How appropriate that this psalm appears in the lectionary readings of Pentecost! Ongoing creation and renewal is what Pentecost is about.

In reflecting on this psalm, Scott Hoezee notes that the Bible tells us that the world is a symphony of praise to the glory of God. In an orchestra, a violinist cannot disdain a flutist; a percussionist cannot sneer at the oboe player. For to play a symphony, the orchestra needs each and every musician and instrument; without the full orchestra, the performance is diminished. In the symphony of creation it is not up to us to determine the relative importance of one species over another. God needs and wants them all to take part; that is why they were put here by God in the first place!

So we cannot shrug our shoulders when we hear that the dusky seaside sparrow has become extinct. We cannot pass over the tragedy by saying, "Well, there are lots of other birds in the world." Instead we should see the creation the way God sees it; as a fundamental whole that needs all of its parts if the rich symphony of God's creation is to be played correctly and beautifully. When a species of bird winks out of existence, God loses a whole section of creation's choir. When forests are clear-cut, there are fewer branches to clap their hands in praise. Because we are created in God's image, "we are the instruments of preservation. It is up to us to keep this part of God's visible glory alive and to let God's praise continue to go forth. 'The heavens declare the glory of God.' Yes, they do. Let's not muffle the chorus."[52]

According to biblical scholar J. Clinton McCann, the poet who wrote psalm 104 was an environmentalist who knew about the intricate interconnectedness and interdependence of air, soil, water, plants, and animals including humans. McCann points out that genuine concern for the environment begins with praising God. To be sure, this sounds hopelessly simplistic, scientifically and technologically naive. But such a starting point and its underlying conviction that the world belongs to God is the only thing that will dislodge our arrogant assumption that we can save the world, as if it were ours to save! In biblical terms, salvation means life, and in biblical terms, the world does not need to be saved! God has already done that. Psalm 104 affirms that God has made every arrangement and provision for the life of

> In the symphony of creation it is not up to us to determine the relative importance of one species over another.

the world. The only problem is if someone disrupts God's design and destroys the delicate balance God has put in place. For the contemporary world, verse 35 may be the key verse in the psalm. To paraphrase this famous verse: we have seen the wicked, and it is us![53]

Surely some serious "soul-searching" is required to determine if we are among those who are responsible for disrupting God's design. The grace of the present moment appears to be that if our answer is "yes," the opportunity is given us to experience *metanoia*, a radical turn-around, which moves us into right relationship with the larger community of creation. Once we experience this relationship and realize that our role is neither to save nor destroy God's sacred work, our voices join the chorus of creation in praise of God: "May the glory of God endure forever." In other words, "May the creation in all its rich and delightful diversity be preserved so that creation's praise chorus will continue."[54]

Photo credit: P. W. Sykes, USFWS

So we cannot shrug our shoulders when we hear that the dusky seaside sparrow has become extinct. We cannot pass over the tragedy....

THE PROPHETIC TRADITION

Isa 11:1-9; 35:1-10; see also 65:17-25

The prophets stand as eloquent and passionate spokespersons for biblical justice. These contemplative women and men see things as God sees them and make known the vision whatever the cost. While they are persistent and courageous in denouncing injustice and its consequences, they also offer a message of hope. These two aspects of the prophetic vocation go hand in hand. One of the expressions of hope is found in the prophetic vision of transformed relationships.

As we listen closely, we hear that the prophets, in their quest for justice, presume the interconnection between humans and the natural world. As Dominican biblical scholar Carol J. Dempsey, O.P. writes,

> Not only do the Israelite prophets show us
> that there is a systemic connection between
> human sinfulness and ecological destruc-

tion, but they also show us through their proclamations that there is an inherent link between creation and redemption, specifically that the redemption of humankind is connected to the restoration of the natural world through a divine promise. This redemption and restoration lead to a vision of a new creation characterized by a return to harmonious relationships between God, ourselves, and the natural world. It is the prophets' eschatological vision that can provide us with a basis for hope and a paradigm for faithful living.[55]

To illustrate the prophetic vision of a new creation, let us look at two familiar passages in the book of Isaiah.

ISAIAH 11:1-9

The first unit of this passage (vv. 1-5) describes the attributes of a new and ideal king from the line of David, a just leader whose character will be shaped by the "spirit of the Lord." The ruler will be concerned especially with the poor. This section has to do with the reign of God in the sociopolitical realm. Christians came to appreciate this passage as the promise of a Messiah who would come and establish peace on Earth.

The second unit (vv. 6-9) is concerned with the reign of God in the order of creation with peace among all creatures. Here we are given a glimpse of the "peaceable kingdom" in which predators and prey, wild and domestic animals, shall live together in peace: wolf with lamb, leopard with kid, calf and fatling with lion. References to the "little child," "the nursing child," and the "weaned child" portray humans as vulnerable, but the child plays safely where the dangerous snake lives. All animals will eat grass/straw (recall that Gen 1:29-31 suggests that in the beginning no animals were carnivores since both humans and animals were given "every kind of green plant for food"). Age-old adversaries are reconciled. All live safely! Verse 9 brings the two units together. The center of the peaceful cosmos is Yahweh's holy mountain where "they will not hurt or destroy." Earth will be full of the knowledge of God as the sea is full of water (v. 9) and that "knowledge" of God leads to *shalom* for all creation. A hope-filled vision!

ISAIAH 35:1-10

Isaiah 35:1-2 describes God changing the desert into a place flourishing with

> We are given a glimpse of the "peaceable kingdom" in which predators and prey, wild and domestic animals, shall live together in peace....

vegetation, a fertile garden, so that the land itself will "rejoice." The arid land will be as glorious with vegetation as fertile Lebanon, Carmel, and Sharon. In verses 3-4, people are urged to strengthen the weak and declare to the fearful that God is coming to save.

In verses 5-7, we hear that human infirmities will be healed, with the eyes of the blind being opened, the ears of the deaf being unstopped, the lame leaping like a deer, the tongue of the speechless singing for joy. And closely connected to this we are told that waters shall break forth in the wilderness and streams in the desert, the burning sand shall become a pool and the thirsty ground springs of water. Verses 1-2 and 6b-7 describing the desert blooming with water and life-giving streams form an *inclusio* around the verses that describe the healing of humans (vv. 3-6a). Humans *and* the natural world come to fullness of life.

> The prophetic vision sees all of God's creation connected and transformed.

Verses 8-10 describe the return of exiles to their homeland. There will be a "Holy Way" where the familiar hazards in the desert of dry land and wild beasts no longer exist; "sorrow and sighing shall flee away." Both the wilderness made fertile and the exiles coming home rejoice and sing! The prophetic

vision sees all of God's creation connected and transformed.

Dempsey provides a stirring, hope-filled reflection on the prophetic eschatological visions:

[They] capture our imaginations, kindle
our spirits, and warm our hearts. It is their
visions that can fill us with amazement and
make us stop and wonder, if we can recover
our wonder, that yes, perhaps there is hope
amidst such disorder and ecological distress
and, yes, the Blue Planet and all that lives
and breathes in it can become, once again,
a safe home for everyone and everything,
with flourishing gardens, land reforested
with baby pines for nestlings and fledglings,
smog-free skies, sea lions swimming with
steel heads in clean waters, wild life roam-
ing and grazing freely without fear of the
hunter's bullet. Perhaps the Blue Planet can
once again be a home with unlocked doors
and unbarred windows where human
beings of all ages and kinds cultivate their
patch of Earth and sit peacefully under a
tree, in simple reverence for other human
beings and all of creation, without forget-
ting that life is a gift, more precious than a
right, and that what needs to be at the heart
of all is "lovingkindness," "compassion,"

because lovingkindness and compassion are at the heart of God, the creator of all life that is good and wholesome and holy.[56]

Isaiah (as well as many other prophets) offers us a reflection on biblical justice and *shalom* that embraces human society *and* the natural order. The prophets of Israel believed that God was still at work, moving creation towards transformed, harmonious relationships. At the same time, the women and men who stood in the prophetic tradition knew that they were not to sit back passively and wait for God to do "God's thing." As contemplatives they were called to see things as God sees them and, in turn, act on that vision. As justice-makers, the prophets were to name by the right name whatever or whoever was disrupting relationships. The prophets were to be about the hard work of transforming broken relationships here and now. And in order to keep hope alive, they offered visions of transformed relationships depicted in rich, powerful, energizing symbolic language.

Biblical scholar Walter Brueggemann describes the prophet as "a destabilizing agent" who issues a gesture or word that intends to play on the imagination of the community. Prophecy is "an assault on public imagination, aimed at showing that the present presumed world is not absolute, but that a thinkable alternative can be imagined, characterized, and lived in."[57] Prophetic visions that picture the "peaceable kingdom" are not presented merely to comfort us but to move us to action, bold prophetic action.

As Christians called to be engaged in prophetic ministry in our world today, we may well listen to the prophetic voices that speak to us across more than two millennia. They remind us that:

- We are called to be contemplative, that is, in touch with God's plan for all creation.

- We cannot separate social justice and eco-justice. All aspects of justice are connected and have to do with right relationship.

- We must be ready to name injustice by the right name, whatever the cost.

- We are challenged to stand up as preachers of the Word and offer creative, bold alternative visions that, on one hand, assault public imagination and, on the other hand, bear hope.

Prophetic visions that picture the "peaceable kingdom" are not presented merely to comfort us but to move us to action, **bold prophetic action.**

Perhaps the Blue Planet
can once again be a home
with unlocked doors and
unbarred windows
where human beings
of all ages and kinds
cultivate their patch of Earth
and sit peacefully under a tree,
in simple reverence
for other human beings
and all of creation....

—Carol J. Dempsey, O.P.

FINAL REFLECTIONS

As I share some of my final reflections on this journey through parts of the Hebrew Bible, I invite you to do the same.

Although I have been aware of the call to biblical justice for quite a few years, I feel that I am a "beginner" as student and as one engaged in the ministry of justice. I say that with excitement as well as awareness of the criticalness and demands of the call. I cannot express how much I am enriched and challenged by study and reflection on the Word of God, complemented and developed these days by a growing appreciation for the New Universe story.

In this "little book" I have tried to open up (certainly not fully develop) some of those biblical insights that are helping me and others to see the interconnectedness of all creation. In simple response to those insights I can say that what stirs my soul is that our God is a God who is bringing forth a good and holy creation and loves it all beyond our imagining. Along with others, I now understand that my "vocation" is a call to help repair broken relationships in the world, in creation. The time in which we live is *kairos* time and I/we cannot afford to dally or offer excuses.

Such awareness not only leads to but insists on concrete responses expressed in lifestyle and ministry. Along with so many others, I can list ways in which I am trying (struggling!) to become more ecologically conscious: recycle but more than that—know where the discards go and the effects they have on others and Earth; use those products that are "Earth-friendly" inside and outside; work against the consumerist mentality that affects me more than I wish to admit (my almost worn out bumper sticker reads: "live simply that others may simply live"); use what I have as long as I can rather than go out and buy the latest and newest; tend Earth; conserve Earth's resources, *e.g.*, water in this part of the country; gather abandoned and abused animals and care for them; re-discover and celebrate Sabbath as time for contemplation that leads to justice-making; contact political officials on issues regarding ecological matters; take every possible opportunity in teaching to show the interrelation between eco-justice and social justice and emphasize that these aspects of justice should never be pitted against each other. I need to be about much, much more but that statement issues from hope not guilt. We do not have time for guilt.

Whatever I try to do to contribute to the well being, the *shalom* of Earth and all she holds, I do as a Dominican woman, a preacher and teacher who walks in the contemplative, prophetic tradition of Dominic and Catherine, in community with others who share the same visions. For the opportunity to be part of such a grand undertaking at this moment in time, I am profoundly grateful to the God who is forever faithful!

Even if our own mouths were as full of song as the sea
- and our lips as full of praise as the breadth of the heavens
- and our eyes as bright as the sun
- and our hands as outstretched as the eagles of the sky
- and our feet as swift as gazelles
we could not thank you enough!

(Sabbath prayer)[58]

EPILOGUE

I began this little book by recalling an experience in my yard with Sunny and young doves. That experience reminds me that I am part of creation right here, right now. Because this awareness is so important in the discussion of our home, Earth, I end this "little book" with a similar experience described by the eloquent spokeswoman on behalf of Earth, Annie Dillard. Her goldfish named Ellery provides this moment of contemplation:

> This Ellery cost me twenty-five cents. He is a deep red-orange, darker than most goldfish. He steers short distances mainly with his slender red lateral fins; they seem to provide impetus for going backward, up, or down. It took me a few days to discover his ventral fins; they are completely transparent and all but invisible dream fins. He also has a short anal fin, and a tail that is deeply notched and perfectly transparent at the two tapered tips. He can extend his mouth

93

so that it looks like a length of pipe; he can shift the angle of his eyes in his head so he can look before and behind himself, instead of simply out to the side.... For this creature, as I said, I paid twenty-five cents. I had never bought an animal before. It was very simple; I went to a store in Roanoke called "Wet Pets"; I handed the man a quarter, and he handed me a knotted plastic bag bouncing with water in which a green plant floated and the goldfish swam. This fish, two bits' worth, has a coiled gut, a spine radiating fine bones, and a brain. Just before I sprinkle his food flakes into his bowl, I rap three times on the bowl's edge; now he is conditioned, and swims to the surface when I rap. And, he has a heart.[59]

NOTES

[1] D. H. Lawrence, POEMS, rev. ed. (New York: Penguin, 1986), pp. 241-42.

[2] Elizabeth A. Johnson, "Passion for God, Passion for the Earth," SPIRITUAL QUESTIONS FOR THE TWENTY-FIRST CENTURY (Maryknoll: Orbis, 2001), p. 119.

[3] *Ibid.*, p. 120.

[4] *Ibid.*, pp. 120-21.

[5] The tensions or distinctions we find between "ecological justice" and "social justice" would be unfamiliar in the biblical world. "Biblical justice" spoke of right relationship between God, humankind, and Earth (the land). This all-encompassing understanding of justice will become evident as we reflect on biblical texts.

[6] Leon Howell, "Ecumenical Earth: An Auburn/Union Conference," UNION NEWS Winter, 1999), pp. 16-19.

[7] Lynn White, Jr., "The Historical Roots of Our Ecological Crisis," SCIENCE 155 (March 10, 1967), pp. 1203-7.

[8] Joseph Sittler, "Evangelism and the Care of the Earth," PREACHING IN THE WITNESSING COMMUNITY, ed. by Herman Stuempfle (Philadelphia: Fortress, 1973), p. 102.

[9] Our focus here is limited to the Hebrew Scriptures. To appreciate fully the topic of ecology and the Bible one will surely wish to continue this study in the New Testament.

[10] See www.TheGreatStory.org, the website of the Rev. Dowd, "an 'evolutionary evangelist', and his wife Connie Barlow, a popular science writer, [who] are full-time itinerant 'Great Story' tellers. They promote 'the marriage of science and religion for personal and planetary well being' by teaching and preaching in colleges, churches, retreat centers, and public and private schools all across North America."

[11] Michael Dowd, "Giving God Glory in Evolution: How Science Will Usher the Church into Its Greatness." Reprinted with permission from the Lent/Easter 2004 issue of Benedictine Bridge, Sisters of Saint Benedict of Madison, Wisconsin.

[12] Bruce Birch, LET JUSTICE ROLL DOWN: THE OLD TESTAMENT, ETHICS, AND CHRISTIAN LIFE (Louisville: Westminster John Knox, 1991), p. 57.

[13] Unless otherwise noted, scriptural quotations will be taken from theNEW REVISED STANDARD VERSION BIBLE (New York: Oxford University Press, 1989).

[14] Richard H. Lowery, SABBATH AND JUBILEE (St. Louis: Chalice Press, 2000), pp. 85-86.

[15] *Ibid*, pp. 82-3.

[16] *Ibid.*, p. 84.

[17] Diane Jacobson, "Biblical Bases for Eco-justice Ethics," THEOLOGY FOR EARTH: A FIELD GUIDE, ed. by Dieter Hessel (Maryknoll: Orbis, 1996), p. 45.

[18] Lowery, pp. 86-87.

[19] Scott Hoezee, REMEMBER CREATION: GOD'S WORLD OF WONDER AND DELIGHT (Grand Rapids: Wm. B. Eerdmans, 1998), pp. 15, 22.

[20] Larry Rasmussen, EARTH COMMUNITY: EARTH ETHICS (Maryknoll: Orbis, 1996), p. 262.

[21] Terence E. Fretheim, "The Book of Genesis," THE NEW INTERPRETER'S BIBLE, vol. 1, ed. by Leander Keck et al. (Nashville: Abingdon, 1994), p. 345.

22 It is worth noting that in the New Testament Jesus says that he "came not to be served but to serve, and to give his life as a ransom for many" (Mark 10:45). This description sheds more light on God's manner of ruling.

23 M. Welker, "What is Creation? Rereading Genesis 1 and 2," THEOLOGY TODAY 48 (1991), p. 64.

24 Maria Harris, PROCLAIM JUBILEE: A SPIRITUALITY FOR THE TWENTY-FIRST CENTURY (Louisville: Westminster John Knox, 1996), pp. 26-27.

25 Harrris quotes Walter Brueggemann, "The Book of Exodus," THE NEW INTERPRETER'S BIBLE, vol. 1, ed. by Leander Keck et al. (Nashville: Abingdon Press, 1994), p. 845.

26 Publication source unknown.

27 Michael J. Himes and Kenneth R. Himes, "The Sacrament of Creation," COMMONWEAL 117 (Jan., 1990), p. 44.

28 Theodore Hiebert, "Rethinking Traditional Approaches to Nature in the Bible," THEOLOGY FOR EARTH COMMUNITY: A FIELD GUIDE, ed. by Dieter Hessel (Maryknoll: Orbis, 1996), pp. 28-29.

29 Elizabeth A. Johnson, WOMEN, EARTH, AND CREATOR SPIRIT (New York: Paulist, 1993), pp. 29-32.

30 Brennan R. Hill, CHRISTIAN FAITH AND THE ENVIRONMENT: MAKING VITAL CONNECTIONS (Maryknoll: Orbis, 1998), pp. 288-89.

31 Mary Elizabeth Moore, MINISTERING WITH THE EARTH (St. Louis: Chalice Press, 1998), pp. 165-67.

32 Himes and Himes, p. 46.

33 Steven Bouma-Prediger, FOR THE BEAUTY OF THE EARTH: A CHRISTIAN VISION FOR CREATION (Grand Rapids: Baker, 2001), p. 98.

34 William French, "Chaos and Creation," THE BIBLE TODAY 33 (Jan. 1995), p. 12.

35 Bouma-Prediger, p. 98.

[36] French, p. 11.

[37] *Ibid.*, pp. 14-15. A comment here on the concept of chaos seems in order. Dominican theologian Cletus Wessels, O.P. (JESUS IN THE NEW UNIVERSE STORY [Maryknoll: Orbis Books, 2003], pp. 182-84) notes that "Our more recent understanding of the Earth, based on our new science, paints a picture of destruction and chaos.... The violent dimensions of earth, air, fire, and water, and the Earth's periodic catastrophes are all examples of order coming out of chaos. The chaos and apparent violence in the universe seem to produce not ultimate destruction, but a new order, a revolutionary leap, new life from death.... The tensions always found within the community of species ultimately lead to an overall balance." Wessels also speaks of "true human violence, evil and sin" that flow from our personal choices. "Humans," Wessels observes, "can act in ways that are contrary to the reign of God.... Human choices can be destructive of our relationships with ourselves, other individuals, human societies, and nature. Human violence is contrary to the evolutionary drive of the Earth because it upsets the ecological balance.... Sin is the tearing of the web of personal relationships, of human societies, and of the community of species." Today this destructive violence that tears the web of relationships may well be understood as the chaos that the stories of Genesis describe as being held at bay.

[38] Fretheim, p. 349.

[39] Jacobson, p. 50.

[40] Raymond C. Van Leeuwen, "The Book of Proverbs," THE NEW INTERPRETER'S BIBLE, vol. 5, ed. by Leander Keck et al. (Nashville: Abingdon, 1997), pp. 92-97.

[41] Jacobson, p. 51.

[42] Mary Catherine Hilkert, O.P., "Bearing Wisdom—the Vocation of the Preacher," SPIRITUALITY TODAY 44 (Summer, 1992), p. 152.

[43] Dianne Bergant, ISRAEL'S WISDOM LITERATURE: A LIBERATION-CRITICAL READING (Minneapolis: Augsburg Fortress, 1997), p. 20.

[44] For popular accounts of the story of the formation of Earth and the universe, see the works of physicist Brian Swimme and cultural historian and Passionist priest Thomas Berry, in particular: THE UNIVERSE STORY (HarperSanFrancisco, 1994).

[45] Bergant, p. 44.

[46] Ibid., pp. 48-49.

[47] Aldo Leopold, SAND COUNTY ALMANAC (New York: Ballantine, 1970), p. 240.

[48] Carol A. Newsom, "The Book of Job,"THE NEW INTERPRETER'S BIBLE, vol. 4, ed. by Leander Keck et al. (Nashville: Abingdon, 1996), pp. 626-27.

[49] Ibid., p. 631.

[50] Bouma-Prediger, p. 105.

[51] E. Kohak, THE EMBERS AND THE STARS: A PHILOSOPHICAL INQUIRY INTO THE MORAL SENSE OF NATURE (Chicago: University of Chicago Press, 1984), pp. 45-46.

[52] Hoezee, pp. 95-96.

[53] J. Clinton McCann, "The Book of Psalms," THE NEW INTERPRETER'S BIBLE, vol. 4, ed. by Leander Keck et al. (Nashville: Abingdon, 1996), pp. 1099-1100.

[54] Hoezee, p. 96.

[55] Carol J. Dempsey, O.P., "Hope Amidst Crisis: A Prophetic Vision of Cosmic Redemption," ALL CREATION IS GROANING: AN INTERDISCIPLINARY VISION FOR LIFE IN A SACRED UNIVERSE, ed. by Carol J. Dempsey and Russell A. Butkus (Collegeville: Liturgical Press, 1999), pp. 270-71.

[56] Dempsey, pp. 276-77.

[57] Walter Brueggemann, A SOCIAL READING OF THE OLD TESTAMENT (Minneapolis: Fortress, 1994), p. 224.

[58] Quoted in the video, KEEPING THE EARTH: RELIGIOUS AND SCIENTIFIC PERSPECTIVES ON THE ENVIRONMENT (Cambridge: Union of Concerned Scientists, 1996).

[59] Annie Dillard, PILCRIM AT TINKER CREEK (New York: HarperCollins, 1974), p. 125.

RECOMMENDED RESOURCES

Below is a list of books, articles, commentaries, and videos that were influential in Sarah Sharkey's thinking and currently inspire her:

Bergant, Dianne. ISRAEL'S WISDOM LITERATURE: A LIBERATION-CRITICAL READING. Minneapolis: Fortress Press, 1997.

Bouma-Prediger, Steven. FOR THE BEAUTY OF THE EARTH: A CHRISTIAN VISION FOR CREATION CARE. Grand Rapids: Baker Book House, 2001.

Hessel, Dieter and Larry Rasmussen, eds. EARTH HABITAT: ECO-JUSTICE AND THE CHURCH'S RESPONSE. Minneapolis: Fortress Press, 2001.

Hill, Brennan R. CHRISTIAN FAITH AND THE ENVIRONMENT: MAKING VITAL CONNECTIONS. Maryknoll: Orbis Books, 1998.

Hoezee, Scott. REMEMBER CREATION: GOD'S WORLD
OF WONDER AND DELIGHT. Grand Rapids: Wm. B.
Eerdmans Publishing Company, 1998.

Johnson, Elizabeth A. "Passion for God, Passion for
the Earth." SPIRITUAL QUESTIONS FOR THE TWENTY-
FIRST CENTURY. Ed. by Mary Hembrow Snyder.
Maryknoll: Orbis Books, 2001. 118-25.

Johnson, Elizabeth A. WOMEN, EARTH, AND CREATOR
SPIRIT. New York: Paulist Press, 1993.

Keck, Leander et al., eds. THE NEW INTERPRETER'S
BIBLE. 12 vols. Nashville: Abingdon Press, 1994-
2001.

Lowery, Richard H. SABBATH AND JUBILEE. St. Louis:
Chalice Press, 2000.

Video: KEEPING THE EARTH: RELIGIOUS AND SCIENTIFIC
PERSPECTIVES ON THE ENVIRONMENT. Cambridge:
Union of Concerned Scientists, 1996.

Beginning in the thirteenth century, a new form of theology emerged in which women, "for the first time in Christianity, took on an important, perhaps even preponderant role," writes Bernard McGinn in the introduction to Meister Eckhart and the Beguine Mystics.[1]

"Vernacular" theology differed both in content and audience from the academic concerns of scholastic theology and the biblical commentary of monastic theology. Written not in Latin but in the spoken language of medieval people, vernacular theology "implied a different and wider audience than that addressed by traditional monastic and scholastic theology."[2]

Among those who contributed significantly to the body of vernacular theology were the Beguines, women in Europe who took up a nontraditional form of independent and apostolic religious life beginning in the twelfth century.

Written by nontraditional women in a nontraditional language, the vernacular teachings also came in nontraditional forms.

According to McGinn, "Much of it was expressed in sermonic form, though of many kinds. A wide variety of treatises and 'little books' were employed..."[3] We draw upon this tradition in publishing this series of "little books," written by

Dominican women in a vernacular created out of the soil of their experience of living into new ways of being human.

For many Catholics, the unfolding "Universe Story" and "new" Earth spirituality are wonder-filled invitations to go deeper into the mysteries of their faith; to plumb its incarnational and sacramental essence. Teilhard de Chardin grasped the awesomeness of it all when he wrote:

> The sacramental Species are formed by the totality of the world, and the duration of the creation is the time needed for its consecration.[4]

Seven hundred years earlier, Beguine mystic Mechtild of Magdeburg (1210-c1280) had intuited this Oneness, writing:

> The day of my spiritual awakening
>   was the day I saw
>   and knew I saw
>   all things in God
>   and God
>   in all things.[5]

More practical than mystical, Sor Juana Inés de la Cruz (1648-1695)—the Mexican nun, scientist, poet, musician, and scholar whose memory is honored by the Sor Juana Press—dedicated herself to "reading" the natural world through observation on the several occasions when she was forbidden to read books. Believing that knowledge of the arts and sciences was the path to knowledge of God, Sor Juana wrote:

> It seem[s] to me debilitating for a Catholic not to know everything in this life of the Divine Mysteries that can be learned through natural means....[6]

It is our hope that these "little books" will stimulate an engaging conversatio ("living with a familiarity that includes but is not limited to verbal discussion"[7]) among women religious and others about both the issues each author presents and the spiritual journey she shares. In particular, we hope that each "little book" will stimulate deep conversatio around questions of faith, spirituality, and Divine consciousness.

- Editors

[1] Meister Eckhart and the Beguine Mystics, ed. by Bernard McGinn (New York: Continuum, 1994), p. 6.
[2] Ibid., p. 8.
[3] Ibid., p. 9.
[4] Pierre Teilhard de Chardin, The Divine Milieu (New York: Harper & Row, Publishers, 1968), p. 126.

[5] Sue Woodruff, Meditations with Mechtild of Magdeburg (Santa Fe, New Mexico: Bear & Company, Inc., 1982), p. 42.

[6] Sor Juana Inés de la Cruz, "Response to the Most Illustrious Poetess Sor Filotea de la Cruz," A Woman of Genius: The Intellectual Autobiography of Sor Juana Inés de la Cruz, trans. by Margaret Sayers Peden (Lime Rock Press, Inc.: Salisbury, Connecticut, 1982), p. 32.

[7] See McGuinn, Meister Eckhart, p. 8, where he refers to "Meister Eckhart's 'conversation' with the Beguines as providing "a particularly instructive example" of ways in which "medieval mystical texts challenge stereotypes about men and women…"

ECOLOGY/ECOSPIRITUALITY CENTERS
Established by Women Religious in the United States
(Known to editors as of February 2004)

ALLIUM
LaGrange Park, Illinois
Sisters of St. Joseph of LaGrange

THE BRIDGE BETWEEN
Denmark, Wisconsin
Sinsinawa Dominican Sisters

CEDAR HILL ENRICHMENT CENTER
Gainsville, Georgia
Adrian Dominican Sisters

CENTER FOR EARTH SPIRITUALITY AND RURAL MINISTRY
Mankato, Minnesota
School Sisters of Notre Dame

CHURCHES' CENTER FOR LAND AND PEOPLE
Sinsinawa, Wisconsin
Sinsinawa Dominican Sisters

CLARE'S WELL
Annandale, Minnesota
Franciscan Sisters of Little Falls

CROWN POINT ECOLOGY CENTER
Bath, Ohio
Sisters of St. Dominic of Akron

CRYSTAL SPRING
Plainville, Massachusetts
Kentucky Dominican Sisters

DOMINICAN REFLECTION CENTER
Edmonds, Washington
Adrian Dominican Sisters

EARTHEART
La Casa de María Retreat Center
Santa Barbara, California
La Casa de María/Immaculate Heart Community
Sisters of St. Joseph, Los Angeles Province
Religious of Sacred Heart of Mary, Western America Province

EARTHLINKS
Denver, Colorado
Loretto Community
Dominican Sisters of Hope

EARTHWORKS
Plymouth, Indiana
Poor Handmaids of Jesus Christ

EVERGREEN
Villa Maria, Pennsylvania
Sisters of Humility of Mary at Villa Maria

FRANCISCAN EARTH LITERACY CENTER
Tiffin, Ohio
Tiffin Franciscans

FRANKLIN FARM
Manchester, New Hampshire
Sisters of Holy Cross

FULL CIRCLE ECOHOUSE OF PRAYER
Port Huron, Michigan
Sisters of Mary Reparatrix

GENESIS FARM
Blairstown, New Jersey
Caldwell Dominican Sisters

GRAILVILLE
Loveland, Ohio
Grailville Community

GREEN MOUNTAIN MONASTERY
North Chittenden, Vermont
Passionist Sisters of the Earth Community

HEARTLAND FARM AND SPIRITUALITY CENTER
Pawnee Rock, Kansas
Great Bend Dominican Sisters

JUBILEE FARM
New Berlin, Illinois
Springfield Dominican Sisters

KNOWLES MERCY SPIRITUALITY CENTER
Waterloo, Nebraska
Sisters of Mercy, Omaha Regional Council

MERCY ECOLOGY INSTITUTE
Madison, Connecticut
Sisters of Mercy

MICHAELA FARM
Oldenburg, Indiana
Sisters of St. Francis of Oldenburg

NAZARETH FARM AND CENTER FOR ENVIRONMENTAL SPIRITUALITY
Kalamazoo, Michigan
Sisters of St. Joseph of Nazareth

PRAIRIE WOODS FRANCISCAN SPIRITUALITY CENTER
Hiawatha, Iowa
Franciscan Sisters of Perpetual Adoration

PRAYER LODGE
Busby, Montana
Sisters of St. Francis of Oldenburg

RED HILL FARM
Acton, Pennsylvania
Sisters of St. Francis of Philadelphia

SANTUARIO SISTERFARM
Welfare, Texas
Adrian Dominican Sisters

SHEPHERD'S CORNER
Blacklick, Ohio
Columbus Dominican Sisters

SIENA SPIRITUALITY CENTER
Water Mill, New York
Amityville Dominican Sisters

SISTERS HILL FARM
Bronx, New York
Sisters of Charity New York

SOPHIA GARDEN AND LEARNING CENTER
Amityville, New York
Amityville Dominican Sisters

SPRINGBANK RETREAT CENTER
Kingstree, South Carolina
Adrian Dominican Sisters
Sisters of St. Francis of Oldenburg

ST. CATHARINE FARM/DOMINICAN EARTH CENTER
St. Catharine, Kentucky
Dominicans of St. Catharine

WATERSPIRIT
Elberon, New Jersey
Sisters of St. Joseph of Peace

WHITE VIOLET CENTER FOR ECO-JUSTICE
Saint Mary-of-the-Woods, Indiana
Sisters of Providence of Saint Mary-of-the-Woods

THE WOODLANDS
Osseo, Wisconsin
Sisters of St. Francis of Assisi

Note: In addition to establishing ecology and/or ecospirituality centers, women religious in the United States and in a number of countries around the world are engaged in an array of activities aimed at conserving land, promoting sustainable practices, restoring natural habitats, and modeling new ways of living lightly on Earth. Descriptions of a number of these efforts can be found on the website of the National Catholic Rural Life Conference (see www.ncrlc.com) and in the annotated directory of members of Sisters of Earth, a network of women dedicated to healing Earth's community of life, founded in 1994 by a group of concerned women religious (see www.sistersofearth.org). As more centers are identified, we will include them in next publication.

Among the many outstanding examples of ecological efforts underway is the "Ecovillage" project completed in April 2003 by the Sisters, Servants of the Immaculate Heart of Mary (IHMs) of Monroe, Michigan. The IHMs invested $56 million in a massive effort to renovate their 376,000-square-foot motherhouse in an environmentally conscious way, developing, among other things, geothermal wells for heating and cooling and a graywater system for reusing water that will cut consumption by thirty-five percent (see www.ihmsisters.org).

Several communities have established congregation-wide ecology committees, such as the Loretto Community's Earth Network Coordinating Committee, to share information, plan ecology projects, sponsor educational events, and motivate the membership to a deeper ecological sensitivity. Some congregations focus on raising ecological consciousness and practices at their motherhouses. For example, the Adrian Dominicans' Earth Stewardship Committee sponsors educational seminars. It also has set up an ecology resource room, coordinated the establishment of a wetlands and a Cosmic Walk on campus grounds, and advocated successfully the switch to chlorine-free post-consumer recycled paper for office supplies.

Others are involved in inter-congregational efforts. In 1998, twelve congregations of women religious, along with other Catholic institutions that own land in the Hudson River bioregion of New York, set up ROAR (Religious Organizations Along the River) to "support one another in using our lands with an attitude of respect for beauty and integrity of Earth" and to "address the interrelated issues of poverty, justice and ecology in this bioregion."